RXpert SERIES Student's Companion

PHARMACEUTICS – I

A Practical Manual

RXpert SERIES
Student's Companion

PHARMACEUTICS – I
A Practical Manual

Pushadapu V V Siva Krishna
M. Pharm, (Ph. D.),
Assistant Professor,
Department of Pharmaceutics,
Vignan Pharmacy College, Vadlamudi,
Guntur, Andhra Pradesh – 522213.

Dr. Puttagunta Srinivasa Babu
M. Pharm, Ph. D.
Professor & Principal,
Vignan Pharmacy College, Vadlamudi,
Guntur, Andhra Pradesh – 522213.

Pharma Med PRESS
An Imprint of BSP Books Pvt. Ltd.

PharmaMed Press
An Imprint of BSP Books Pvt. Ltd.
4-4-309/316, Giriraj Lane,
Sultan Bazar, Hyderabad - 500 095.

Pharmaceutics – I: A Practical Manual

by Pushadapu V V Siva Krishna and Dr. Puttagunta Srinivasa Babu

Published by

PharmaMed Press

An Imprint of BSP Books Pvt. Ltd.

4-4-309/316, Giriraj Lane, Sultan Bazar, Hyderabad - 500 095.

Phone: 040-23445688; Fax: 91+40-23445611

E-mail: info@pharmamedpress.com

www.pharmamedpress.com/pharmamedpress.net

ISBN: 978-93-48734-71-6 (Hardback)

Preface

Pharmaceutics - I hold significant importance as a foundational subject in the first year of the B. Pharm. program. Presenting this book to our readers is a source of immense satisfaction. The content of the book is meticulously crafted to align with the syllabus outlined by the Pharmacy Council of India (PCI). Throughout this manual, you will find detailed protocols, safety guidelines, and insightful background information to enhance your understanding of each experiment. It is essential to follow the procedures outlined in each experiment meticulously, paying close attention to details and recording your observations accurately. The laboratory experience is not only an opportunity to apply theoretical knowledge but also a chance to develop critical thinking, problem-solving, and laboratory skills that are essential for your future practice as a pharmacist.

We express our sincere gratitude to Hon. Dr. Lavu Rathaiah Garu, the esteemed founder chairman of the Vignan Group of Institutions, for his unwavering encouragement. Our heartfelt thanks go to Lavu Srikrishna Devarayalu Garu, Vice Chairman of the Vignan Group of Institutions, for his consistent and uplifting support. I extend my sincere gratitude to Dr. P. Srinivasa Babu, Professor & Principal at Vignan Pharmacy College, Vadlamudi, Guntur, for his significant contributions to this book. I am truly thankful for the freedom he granted me to work and for his motivating presence throughout the process.

A heartfelt appreciation goes to my wife, Mrs. Alahari Saranya, whose unwavering motivation has been the driving force behind my passion for writing books. Her constant support and encouragement have been invaluable throughout this journey. I am also deeply grateful for the boundless energy provided by my son, Chetan Krithvik – a true energy pill in my life. Additionally, I extend my sincere gratitude to my parents for their blessings, which have played a pivotal role in the successful completion of this book. Without All unwavering support & blessings, this achievement would not have been possible.

Authors

Contents

GOOD LABORATORY PRACTICES

GLP establishes standard operating procedures and quality control measures for laboratories conducting various tests on physical, chemical, and microbial materials.

Its primary objective is to ensure the accuracy, reliability, and reproducibility of test results while minimizing risks to human health and safety.

SPECIFIC SAFETY GUIDELINES:

Prohibited Activities:

Smoking, eating, drinking, and applying cosmetics in the laboratory are strictly prohibited.

Emergency Preparedness:

Be familiar with the location and operation of firefighting equipment and emergency exits.

Personal Protective Equipment (PPE):

Always wear designated laboratory coats, safety glasses, gloves, and other protective clothing based on the specific hazards encountered.

Chemical Labeling and Handling:

Ensure all containers are clearly labeled with content, safety information, and hazard symbols. This is especially crucial for poisonous and flammable substances.

Compressed Gas Safety:

Follow established protocols for handling and securing gas cylinders to prevent accidents.

First-Aid and Antidotes:

Readily available first-aid supplies, instructions on their use, and specific antidotes for relevant chemicals are essential.

Resource Conservation:

Turn off utilities (air, gas, water) when not in use to conserve resources and minimize safety risks.

Buddy System:

Avoid working alone in the laboratory. Have a designated partner present for safety and collaboration.

Work Environment Maintenance:

Maintain a clean and organized workspace, including laboratory benches and equipment. This minimizes clutter and potential hazards

LABORATORY SAFETY

- Always wear closed-toe shoes and a lab coat for protection.
- Report spills/accidents immediately to your instructor.
- Learn the location and use of safety equipment (first meeting!).
- No eating, drinking, smoking, or solo work in the lab.
- Properly dispose of chemicals in designated containers (not the sink!).
- Keep your workspace clean and organized.

Eye Protection is Key:

- Wear safety glasses always, even over regular glasses.
- Contact lenses? Leave them out of the lab.

Handle Chemicals Wisely:

- Follow instructions on labels and from your instructor.
- Prevent skin and clothing contact with chemicals.
- Clean up spills promptly, especially near balances and reagents.
- Cap containers immediately after use.
- Limit inhalation of organic solvent vapors, especially aromatics and chlorinated ones.

Dispose of Waste Responsibly:

- Follow experiment-specific disposal instructions.
- Flush water-soluble substances with plenty of water if allowed.
- Place insoluble waste in designated containers based on their type.

Remember: Safety is everyone's responsibility. Be aware, follow the rules, and enjoy a safe and productive lab experience!

Common Laboratory Apparatus

Materials Required for Pharmaceutics – I Laboratory

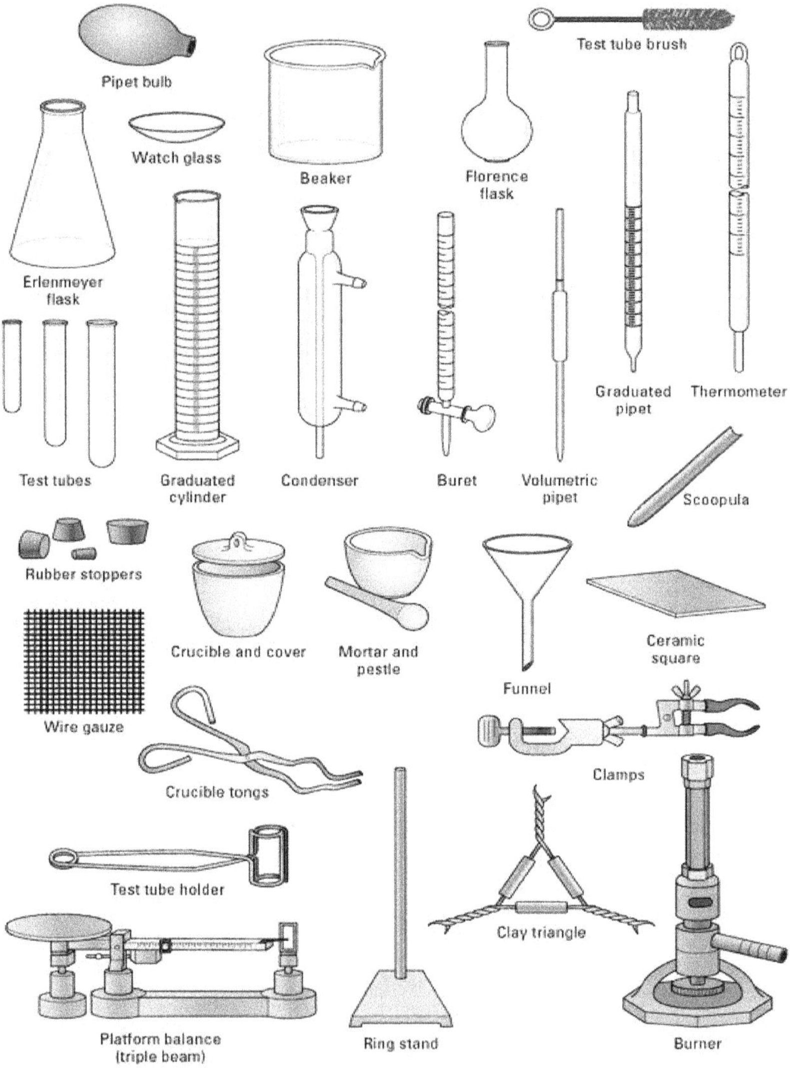

Every student is required to have a compact bag containing essential materials for conducting experiments. Regular checks and maintenance of the bag are mandatory. The bag should include the following items.

1. Clean White Apron
2. Practical Record Book

3. Pencil, Eraser, Ruler, Sharpener
4. Glass Marker Pen
5. Butter Paper
6. Napkin
7. Self-adhesive labels of different size
8. Scientific Calculator
9. Bond Papers
10. Match Box/lighter

General Label Format for a Manufactured Dosage Form in the Laboratory:

Name of the Dosage Form (ml)		
CATEGORY: STORAGE: (Generally, Store in a well-closed container at a temperature notexceeding 25°C) PRECAUTION:	Name of the Ingredients with quantity Manufactured by: (Name of the institution)	Lic.no._______ Mfg. Date: Batch no._____ Expiry date

Examination Pattern:

In all pharmacy institutions across India, the curriculum adheres to the Pharmacy Council of India (PCI) Syllabus, organized in a semester pattern for examinations. For a practical examination with a total of 50 marks, the marking scheme comprises 15 marks for internal assessment and 35 marks for external examination. A predetermined set of criteria governs the allocation of marks for both internal and external assessments. The breakdown of the subject matter and its correlation with marks is as follows:

S. No	Criteria	Internal*	External
1	Synopsis	10	05
2	Experiment	25	25
3	Viva – Voce	05	05
Total		40	35

* Internal Examination is conducted for 40 Marks and obtained marks are reduce.

List of Experiments

1. **Syrups**
   (a) Syrup IP"66
   (b) Compound syrup of Ferrous phosphate BPC"68
2. **Elixirs**
   (a) Piperazine paediatric elixir
   (b) Paracetamol paediatric elixir
3. **Linctus**
   (a) Terpin Hydrate Linctus IP'66
   (b) Iodine Throat Paint (Mandle's Paint)
4. **Solutions**
   (a) Strong solution of ammonium acetate
   (b) Cresol with soap solution
5. **Suspensions**
   (a) Calamine lotion
   (b) Magnesium hydroxide mixture
   (c) Aluminium Hydroxide gel
6. **Emulsions**
   (a) Turpentine liniment
   (b) Liquid paraffin emulsion
7. **Powders and granules**
   (a) ORS powder (WHO)
   (b) Effervescent granules
   (c) Dusting powder
   (d) Divided powders
8. **Suppositories**
   (a) Glycero gelatin suppository
   (b) Cocoa butter suppository
   (c) Zinc oxide suppository
9. **Semisolids**
   (a) Sulphur ointments

(b) Non-staining iodine ointment with methyl salicylate

(c) Carbopol gel

10. Gargles and Mouth washes

(a) Iodine gargle

(b) Chlorhexidine Mouth wash

LIST OF ABBREVATIONS:

IP	Indian pharmacopeia
USP	United states pharmacopeia
BP	British pharmacopeia
NF	National formulary
q. s	Quantity sufficient
BHT	Butylated hydroxyl toluene
EDTA	Ethylene diamine tetra acetic acid
PEG	Polyethylene glycol
BHA	Butylated hydroxyl anisole
SLS	Sodium lauryl sulphate
HPMC	Hydroxyl propyl methyl cellulose
MCC	Microcrystalline cellulose
WHO	World health organization
ORS	Oral Rehydration solution
BPC	Bulk pharmaceutical chemical
DV	Displacement value
GIT	Gastro intestinal tract
HLB	Hydrophilic lipophilic balance
API	Active pharmaceutical ingredients
MP	Melting point
gm	Grams
ml	Millilitres
mg	Milligrams

INTRODUCTION TO DRUG & DOSAGE FORM:

Drug:

The drug is also called an "API" (Active Pharmaceutical Ingredient).

It is an Agent intended for diagnosis, mitigation, cure/prevention of any type of disease in Humans (or) Animals.

- API - is only responsible for pharmacological (or) Therapeutic Activity in the Body.

DOSAGE FORM:

"Drug (or) API" +"Excipients" ⟶ Dosage form.

- Drugs are not administered to patients directly in their original form.
- So, they are converted into Dosage forms with or without excipients.
- Excipients are also called "Additives'
- These are "Inert Substances" that do not have any therapeutic (or) pharmacological Activity in the Body.

Examples of Excipients:

Diluents, Disintegrants, Binders, Lubricants, Glidants, Solvents, Coloring Agents, Sweetening Agents, Flavouring Agents etc.

Examples of Dosage forms:

Tablets, Syrups, Capsules, Suspensions, Emulsions, Pastes, Ointments, Creams etc.

All Dosage Forms Contain one (or) more Active Pharmaceutical Ingredients along with (Or) without Excipients.

NECESSITY OF FORMULATION OF DOSAGE FORMS: -

- Dosage forms Contribute to patient compliance and acceptance.
- Dosage forms should be convenient to use, handle, and store.
- The dosage form should provide an accurate dose suitable for every age group.
- It should be economical, and its presentation should be elegant.
- The formulation should be able to mask the bitter taste and bad odor of the drug.
- It should protect the drug from degradation under *in vivo* acidic conditions, such as enteric-coated tablets.
- Dosage forms should allow easy administration of the drug into various body cavities like the rectum or vagina.
- They should prevent the degradation of the drug from environmental conditions such as moisture, oxygen, and light.

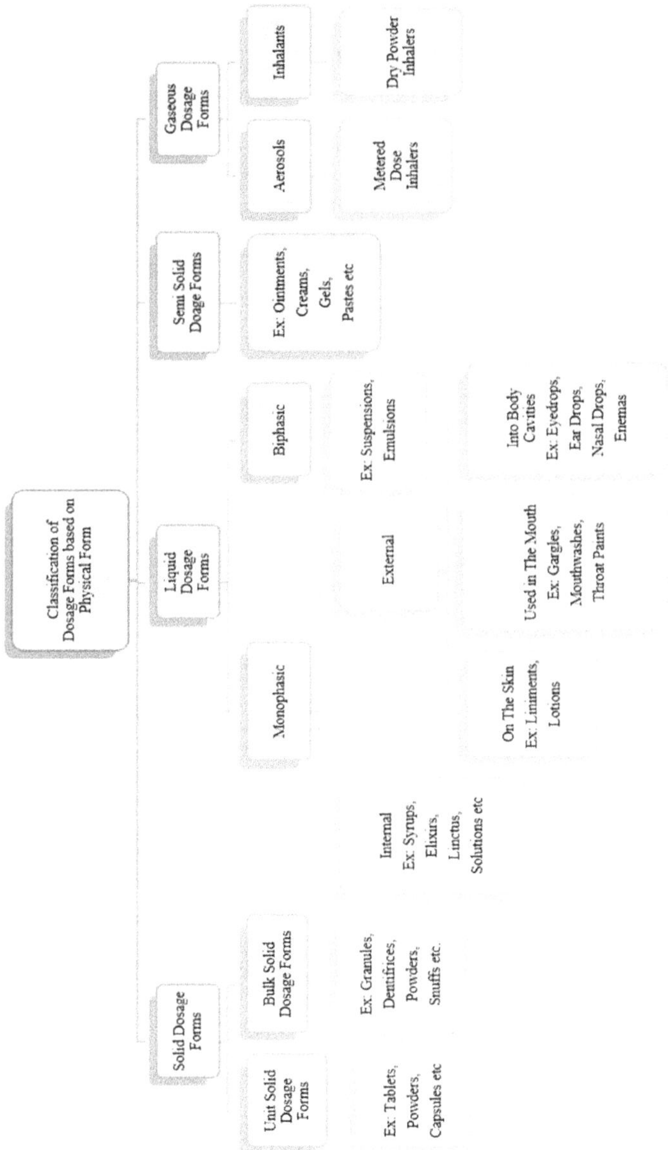

Classification of Pharmaceutical Dosage Forms based on their Physical Nature

Latin terms / Phrase Abbreviations Used in Pharmaceutics

Latin terms / Phrase Abbreviations:

Latin term	Abbreviation	Meaning in English
Semel in die (or) omne in die	o.d	Once a day.
Bis in die, Bis die	b.d	Twice a day
Ter in die, ter die	Tid / t.d	Thrice a day
Quartar in die	q.i.d: q.d	Four times a day
Sexies in die	Sex. i.d	Six times a day
Si opus sit	s.o.s	When required
a.c	Ante cibum	Before meals
p.c	Post cibum	After meals

Dosage form related Latin terms / Phrase Abbreviations:

Latin term	Abbreviation	Meaning in English
Capsulo	caps	A capsule
Charta	chart	A powder
Cremor	crem	A cream
Emulsio	emul	An emulsion
Gelatina	gelat	A jelly
Gutlae	gtl	drops
Inhalatio	inhal	An inhalation
Injectio	inj	An injection
liquor	liq	A solution
lotio	lot	A lotion
naristillae	narist	Nasal drops
pasta	past	A paste
pilula	pil	A pill
pulvis	puly	A powder
pulvis	Puly	A dusting
tabella	tab	A tablet
pessaries		A suppository

CHAPTER – 1

SYRUPS – INTRODUCTION

Definition: syrups are defined as pharmaceutical preparations containing one or more active ingredients dissolved or suspended in a concentrated aqueous solution of sugar or a sugar substitute. These preparations are typically used for oral administration and are intended to be palatable and easy to swallow. Syrups in pharmacopeial standards must meet specific quality criteria regarding their composition, stability, and packaging to ensure their efficacy and safety for medicinal use.

FORMULATORY INGREDIENTS

The formulation of syrups can vary depending on their intended use, but some common ingredients used in their preparation include:

Sugar: Typically, sucrose, but sometimes other sugars or sugar substitutes like glucose or fructose are used.

Water: Used as the solvent for dissolving the sugar and other ingredients.

Flavors: Natural or artificial flavors such as fruit extracts, essential oils, or synthetic flavor compounds are added to impart desired taste.

Preservatives: Substances like benzoic acid, sorbic acid, or sodium benzoate may be included to prevent microbial growth and extend the shelf life of the syrup.

Colorants: Optional color additives may be used to enhance the appearance of the syrup, especially if it's flavored with fruits or herbs.

Thickening agents: These can include natural thickeners like agar, pectin, or gum Arabic to adjust the viscosity of the syrup.

Acidulants: Citric acid or other acids may be added to adjust the pH of the syrup and enhance its flavor.

Medicinal Ingredients: In pharmaceutical syrups, active pharmaceutical ingredients (APIs) are added in specific concentrations to provide therapeutic effects.

CLASSIFICATION OF SYRUPS:

Simple Syrups:

- Simple syrups are basic syrups made by dissolving sugar in water over heat until the sugar is completely dissolved.
- These syrups are primarily used as sweeteners in beverages and desserts.
- Simple syrups are versatile and can serve as a base for flavored syrups or be infused with additional ingredients for various culinary purposes.

Medicated Syrups:

- Medicated syrups are pharmaceutical preparations containing active medicinal ingredients dissolved or suspended in a syrup base.
- They are formulated to deliver specific therapeutic effects and are often used for oral administration.
- Common examples include cough syrups, antacids, expectorants, and other over-the-counter or prescription medications.

Flavored Syrups:

- Flavored syrups are syrups infused with natural or artificial flavors to enhance taste and aroma.
- These syrups can be used in both culinary and beverage applications to add flavor and sweetness.
- Flavored syrups are available in a wide variety of flavors, including fruits (e.g., strawberry, raspberry), herbs (e.g., mint, lavender), spices (e.g., cinnamon, vanilla), and specialty flavors (e.g., caramel, chocolate).

Preparation of Syrups:

Simple Solution method with the help of heat: -

This method is used when the substances are thermostable and non-volatile in nature.

Ex: - Simple Syrup., Tolu Syrup N.F., cocoa syrup N.F act.It is less time-consuming method

Simple solution method by agitation: - [without heat]

This method is suitable for thermolabile substances and volatile substances.

- Syrups prepared by this method have maximum stability.

  Ex: Ephedrine sulphate syrup. Codeine phosphate syrup.

Percolation [extraction] method:

In this method, Sucrose is percolated with purified water as a menstrum.

Ex: Tolu Syrup Squill Syrup.

Advantages:

- Syrups retard the oxidation of drugs; because sucrose itself gets hydrolyzed to laevulose and dextrose which are reducing sugars.
- They are sweet in taste. Therefore, bitter taste of drugs can be reduced.
- Syrups prevent microbial decomposition of many vegetable drugs.

Disadvantages:

- On continuous intake syrups promote dental decay and cause gingivitis because it is a very good supplement for bacterial growth
- Syrups are not suitable for diabetic patients and patients who are on a restricted calorie intake.
- Aluminum salts cannot be included in syrups as these are incompatible with sucrose
- Syrups are not suitable for acidic drugs as they promote crystallization of sucrose.

Date: **Experiment - 01**

SIMPLE SYRUP IP'66

Aim: To prepare and submit Simple Syrup IP

Type of product: Syrup

Category: Sweetened vehicle, Pharmaceutical aid

Composition: Sucrose 66.67% w/w (IP) or 85% w/v (USP)

Apparatus: Glass beaker, glass rod, measuring cylinders, spatula, dispensing balance.

Principle: Syrups are concentrated aqueous preparations of sucrose or sugar substitutes with or without flavoring agents and medicinal substances. Syrup USP is 66.7% w/v solution of sucrose in 33.3% of purified water as the solvent prepared by simple dissolution with the aid of heat. Simple syrups do not contain active ingredients. They are not intended to be administered as such but are used as vehicle for their flavoring and sweetening properties.Syrups should be freshly prepared (extemporaneous preparation) unless they contain suitable anti-microbial properties. Syrup IP has optical rotation of +56° to +60°.

The solubility of sucrose is 1 in 0.5 parts of water. The quantity of water 33.3% is just enough to dissolve sucrose. Heating enhances the solubility and reduces the viscosity of syrup which permits proper stirring. During preparation, boiling water is added to compensate the water loss by evaporation and to adjust weight. But excess water should not be used to prepare syrup because this leads dilution of concentration of syrup which in turn prone to microbial attack. Moreover, excessive heating is restrained to prevent inversion of sucrose.

$$C_{12}H_{22}O_{11} \xrightarrow{H_2O} 2\ C_6H_{12}O_6$$

Invert sugar so formed readily gets fermented and cause brown coloration to the product. The concentration 66.67% w/w of sucrose doesn't provide microbial growth due to high osmotic pressure is present in saturated solution of sucrose.

Procedure:

1. Add water to sucrose in a tared beaker and heat on a water bath until sucrose dissolves.
2. Add sufficient boiling water to produce sufficient quantity.
3. Filter hot syrup if it is not clear. Cool. (0.15% methyl paraben may be added as preservative)

Storage: Store in a cool and dark place.

Simple Syrup Formula:

S. No	Ingredients	Quantity Given	Quantity Taken (factor X quantity given)
1	Sucrose	667 g	
2	Purified water q. s	1000 g	

Calculations:

Factor = Required quantity/Quantity Given

LABEL

(Students shall write all aspects of labelling in the space provided below)

SIMPLE SYRUP, IP. (ml)		
USE: Pharmaceutical aid **STORAGE:** Store in a well closed container at a temperature not exceeding 25°C	A non-medicated syrup contains: Sucrose:66.7% w/w Wt. Per ml:1.315 to 1.317 Name of the institution	Lic.no.________ Mfg. Date:_____ Batch no._______ Expiry date _____

Report:

Date: **Experiment - 02**

COMPOUND SYRUP OF FERROUS PHOSPHATE BPC'68

Aim: To prepare and submit 25 ml of Compound Ferrous Phosphate syrup.

Synonyms: Parish food or parish syrup or chemical food.

Type of product: Syrup

Category: Haematinic.

Composition: Iron 0.4% w/v, Calcium 0.5% w/v.

Dose: 2 to 8ml

Apparatus: Glass beaker, glass rod, measuring cylinders, spatula, dispensing balance.

Principle: Diet with insufficient supply of iron leads to a condition called anaemia. In such cases, iron supplement, ferrous phosphate syrup is prescribed. Ferrous phosphate syrup is a preparation containing iron along with electrolytes, calcium, potassium, and sodium. These electrolytes overcome the deficiency which is most common in anemic condition. Ferrous phosphate is prepared by a reaction between iron and phosphoric acid. The reaction is expressed in the following equations.

1. Preparation of ferrous acid phosphate.

$$Fe + 2H_3PO_4 \longrightarrow Fe(H_2PO_4) + H_2 \uparrow$$

Allign as per above reaction

1. Iron
2. Phosphoric acid
3. Ferrous acid Phosphate

Electrolytes are also supplied in their phosphate form. The reaction between phosphoric acid and calcium carbonate, potassium carbonate, sodium phosphate are as follows. This syrup contains 0.4 -0.45% of iron and 0.5 – 0.58% w/v of calcium. This syrup is prepared by chemical reaction method. The chemical reactions involved in the preparation of syrup are as follows:

2. Preparation of solution containing acid phosphate of calcium, potassium and sodium.

$$CaCO_3 + 2H_3PO_4 \longrightarrow Ca(H_2PO_4)2 + H_2O + CO_2 \uparrow$$

These move to above under reaction
1. Calcium carbonate
2. Phosphoric acid
3. Calcium acid Phosphate

$$KHCO_3 + H_3PO_4 \longrightarrow KH_2PO_4 + H2O + CO2 \uparrow$$

1. Potassium bicarbonate
2. Phosphoric acid
3. Potassium acid Phosphate

$$NaHPO_4 + H_3PO_4 \longrightarrow 2NaH_2PO_4$$

1. Sodium Hydrogen Phosphate
2. Phosphoric acid
3. Sodium acid Phosphate

The reactions do not complete at this stage, because the amount of phosphoric acid is insufficient. Hence, excess of phosphoric acid is included in the formula to complete the reactions.

Aqueous extract of Colchineal acts as a coloring agent. It also acts as a masking agent to mask color change of the preparation during storage due to oxidation of constituents. Orange flower water acts as flavoring agent. Since iron is essentially supplied orally, syrup (sucrose) is used as a major ingredient as sweetening agent.

This preparation is a Haematinic and is used in iron deficiency.

Procedure:

Part -1: Preparation of medicinal contents:

1. Phosphoric acid is diluted with water and divided into 2 portions.
2. To one portion of diluted phosphoric acid, iron is added. The contents are heated on a water bath until iron dissolves. Heating on a water bath minimizes evaporation of water. If evaporation of water takes place, a solid mass is formed, which will not dissolve in water.
3. Calcium carbonate, potassium bicarbonate and sodium phosphate are dissolved in a second portion of diluted phosphoric acid in a beaker by stirring. Carbon dioxide (effervescence) is allowed to evolve.
4. The contents of 2nd step are mixed with the contents of 3rd step.

5. The reactions are completed. The resulting solution contains impurities like ironcarbide, which are derived from the iron solution. The contents are filtered to remove these unwanted substances.

Part-2: Preparation of vehicle:

1. Coloring agent is extracted from Colchineal by boiling it for 15 minutes with water.
2. Sugar is added to the above-colored solution and heating is continued until sugar completely dissolves.
3. The hot syrup containing coloring agent is cooled, strained and washed with water to produce a specified volume.

Part-3: Mixing of part 1 and 2:

1. The colored syrup is now mixed with mixture containing medicaments.
2. To the above mixture orange flower water is added and the final volume is adjusted with water.
3. The contents are transferred into a tightly closed container, capped, labelled and submitted.

Storage: Store in a tightly closed container in a cool place.

Formulation table:

S. No.	Ingredients	Quantity Given	Quantity Taken (factor X quantity given)
1.	Iron	4.3g	
2.	Phosphoric acid	80ml	
3.	Calcium carbonate	13.6g	
4.	Sodium phosphate	1.0g	
5.	Potassium bicarbonate	1.0g	
6.	Colchineal	3.5g	
7.	Sucrose	700g	
8.	Orange flower water	50ml	
9.	Purified water q.s	1000ml	

Calculations:

Factor = Required quantity/Quantity Given

Label: (Students shall write all aspects of labelling in the space provided below)

COMPOUND SYRUP OF FERROUS PHOSPHATE		
USE: Iron and electrolyte supplement STORAGE: Store in a tightly closed container in a cool place.	A medicated syrup contains: Iron 0.4% w/v, Calcium 0.5% w/v. **Dose:2** to 8ml Name of the institution	Lic.no.________ Mfg. Date:_____ Batch no.______ Expiry date ____

Report:

CHAPTER - 2

ELIXIRS- INTRODUCTION

An elixir is a clear, sweetened, hydroalcoholic liquid Preparation intended for oral use. Elixirs typically contain one or more active pharmaceutical ingredients (APIs) dissolved or dispersed in a hydroalcoholic solvent system, along with suitable flavoring agents, sweeteners, and other excipients. They are formulated to provide a palatable and stable dosage form for administering medications orally. Elixirs are commonly used in pharmacy practice for delivering drugs that are poorly soluble in water or for masking the taste of bitter or unpleasant-tasting drugs.

CLASSIFICATION:

Non- Medicated Elixirs: - The elixirs which does not have any API and have only excipients are called non-medicated elixirs

These doesn't have any pharmaceutical / therapeutic activity.

Ex: Simple elixir. Flavored elixir.

Medicated Elixirs: - The elixirs containing potent drugs such as antibiotics, antihistamines (or) sedatives are called medicated elixirs.

Ex: piperazine citrate elixir Paracetamol elixir.

FORMULATION INGREDIENTS:

Active Pharmaceutical Ingredients (APIs):

- These are the medicinal substances intended to provide the therapeutic effect. The concentration of APIs in the elixir formulation is determined based on the desired dose per unit volume.

Solvent System:

- Elixirs commonly use a hydroalcoholic solvent system, which consists of a mixture of water and alcohol. The choice of solvent system depends on factors such as solubility of the APIs and desired stability of the formulation.

- The alcohol component, typically ethanol, acts as a co-solvent to improve the solubility of lipophilic drugs and aids in preserving the formulation.
- The ratio of water to alcohol can vary depending on the specific requirements of the formulation.

Sweeteners:

- To enhance palatability, elixirs often contain sweetening agents such as sucrose, sorbitol, glycerin, or artificial sweeteners like saccharin.
- The sweetener helps mask the bitter taste of some APIs and improves overall Taste.

Flavoring Agents:

- Flavoring agents are added to elixirs to improve odour and mask any unpleasant flavors associated with the APIs or other ingredients.
- Common flavoring agents include natural extracts, essential oils, and synthetic flavors.

Preservatives:

- Preservatives may be included in elixir formulations to prevent microbial growth and ensure stability throughout the shelf life of the product.
- Common preservatives used in elixirs include benzoic acid, sorbic acid, sodium benzoate, and parabens.

Colorants (optional):

- Colorants may be added to elixirs to enhance appearance and facilitate product identification. However, they are generally optional and may not be included in all formulations.

Other Excipients:

- Additional excipients such as viscosity modifiers, antioxidants, pH adjusters, and stabilizers may be incorporated into elixir formulations as needed to improve product quality, stability, and manufacturability.

Date: **Experiment - 3**

PIPERAZINE CITRATE ELIXIR IP

Aim: To prepare and submit 20 ml of Piperazine Citrate elixir IP.

Type of product: Medicated elixir

Category: Anthelmintic.

Composition: Each 5ml contains 0.9gm of Piperazine citrate.

Dose: 4 – 15 ml for thread worms daily in divided doses; up to 30ml as a single dose for round worms.

Principle: Piperazine citrate elixir is used as anthelmintic to expel the worms from the intestine. The medicinal agent, Piperazine citrate is a salt form and is soluble in the vehicle, purified water. Chloroform spirit acts as a preservative. Orange oil acts as flavoring agent. Glycerin acts as a co-solvent to enhance the solubility of drug.

Piperazine citrate has unpleasant acid taste; hence sweetening agent like simple syrup is used to mask the taste of the drug. However, chloroform spirit, glycerin and orange oil also help in masking the taste of the drug.

Procedure:

1. Accurately weigh the required quantity of Piperazine citrate and dissolved in $3/4^{th}$quantity of purified water.
2. Mix orange oil with chloroform spirit and add it into the Piperazine citrate solution and mix well.
3. Add syrup and glycerin to the above solution and mix well.
4. Finally make up the volume with purified water and mix it well and keep it aside for few minutes.
5. The preparation is filtered, if necessary and then transferred into a suitable container.

Storage: Store in a tightly closed container in a cool and dark place.

Formula:

S. No.	Ingredients	Quantity Given	Quantity taken
1	Piperazine citrate	18.0gm	
2	Chloroform spirit	0.5ml	
3	Glycerin	10ml	
4	Orange oil	0.025ml	
5	Simple syrup	50ml	
6	Purified Water	q.s to 100ml	

Calculations:

Label: (Students shall write all aspects of labelling in the space provided below)

PIPERAZINE CITRATE ELIXIR IP		
USE: Anthelmintic. **STORAGE:** Store in a well closed container at a temperature not exceeding 25°C	A elixir Each 5ml contains 0.9gm of Piperazine citrate. Dose: 4 – 15 m Name of the institution	Lic.no.________ Mfg. Date:_____ Batch no.______ Expiry date ____

Report:

Date: **Experiment - 04**

PARACETAMOL PEDIATRIC ELIXIR

Aim: To prepare and submit 25 ml of Paracetamol pediatric elixir BPC.

Category: Analgesic, Antipyretic.

Composition: Paracetamol – 2.4% w/v.

Dose: 5 – 10ml.

Apparatus: Glass beaker, glass rod, measuring cylinders, spatula, dispensing balance.

Principle: This is a preparation containing 2.4% w/v of paracetamol in a suitable flavored vehicle. Paracetamol acts as an analgesic and anti-pyretic with mild anti-inflammatory activity. Since paracetamol is sparingly soluble in water, alcohol and propylene glycol are used to increase ions solubility. Invert syrup contains a mixture of glucose, fructose and may be prepared by hydrolyzing sucrose with a mineral acid such as hydrochloric acid and neutralizing the solution with calcium carbonate or sodium carbonate. Invert syrup when mixed in suitable proportions with syrup prevents the deposition of crystals of sucrose duringstorage. It is also used as sweetening agent to mask the bitter taste of the drug.

Chloroform spirit is the preservative. Raspberry juice is the flavoring agent. Amaranth solution is the coloring agent. Glycerin is the vehicle and also increases the viscosity of the preparation.

Procedure:

1. Paracetamol was dissolved in a mixture of alcohol, propylene glycol and chloroform spirit with stirring.
2. Concentrated raspberry juice is dissolved in invert syrup and amaranth solution were added to the above solution and mixed well.
3. Sufficient glycerin was added to produce the required volume.

Storage: Store in a well-closed container in a cool place.

Formulation table:

S. No.	Ingredients	Quantity Given	Quantity Taken (factor X quantity given)
1.	Paracetamol	2.4gm	
2.	Alcohol 90%	10ml	
3.	Propylene glycol	10ml	
4.	Conc. Raspberryjuice	2.5ml	
5.	Chloroform	2ml	
6.	Invert syrup	28ml	
7.	Amaranth solution	0.2ml	
8.	Glycerin	100ml	

Calculations:

Factor = Required quantity/Quantity Given

PARACETAMOL PEDIATRIC ELIXIR		
USE: Analgesic, Antipyretic. STORAGE: Store in a well-closed container in a cool place.	A pediatric elixir contains: Paracetamol – 2.4% w/v. Dose: 5 – 10ml. Name of the institution	Lic.no._______ Mfg. Date:____ Batch no. _____ Expiry date. ____

Report:

CHAPTER – 3

LINCTUSES-INTRODUCTION

"Linctus" is a term used in pharmacy to refer to a liquid medicine, often syrup-based, that is formulated to soothe or relieve symptoms associated with respiratory conditions such as coughs and sore throats. Linctuses typically contain active ingredients such as cough suppressants, expectorants, antiseptics, or soothing agents, along with sweeteners and flavorings to enhance palatability. They are commonly available over the counter and may be prescribed by healthcare professionals for symptomatic relief of coughing or throat irritation. Linctuses are administered orally, usually in measured doses using a spoon or a calibrated cup, and are designed to provide temporary relief from coughing and associated discomfort. They come in a variety of formulations tailored to different age groups and specific symptoms, making them a popular choice for managing respiratory ailments in both children and adults.

Excipients used in Linctus Preparation:

Linctuses typically contain various excipients (inactive ingredients) that serve different purposes in the formulation. Here are some common excipients used in linctuses:

Sweeteners: Such as sucrose, glucose, or fructose, are often added to improve the taste and palatability of the linctus, making it more pleasant to consume.

Flavorings: These can include natural or artificial flavors like cherry, menthol, lemon, or honey, which help mask the odour and sometimes-unpleasant taste of active ingredients and sweeteners.

Preservatives: To prevent microbial growth and extend the shelf life of the linctus, preservatives such as sodium benzoate, potassium sorbate, or alcohol may be added.

Thickeners: These helps give the linctus its syrupy consistency and improve its viscosity for easier administration. Common thickeners include glycerin, carboxymethylcellulose (CMC), or xanthan gum.

Humectants: To help retain moisture and prevent the linctus from drying out, humectants like propylene glycol or sorbitol may be included in the formulation.

Stabilizers: These ingredients help maintain the stability and uniformity of the linctus over time, preventing separation or precipitation of its components. Examples include polysorbate 80 or methylcellulose.

Colorants: Sometimes added to enhance the appearance of the linctus or to differentiate between different flavors or formulations. These can be natural or artificial food colorings.

Antioxidants: To prevent oxidation and maintain the quality of the linctus, antioxidants like ascorbic acid (vitamin C) or sodium metabisulfite may be included.

Purified Water: Used as a solvent to dissolve and dilute the active ingredients and excipients, forming the bulk of the linctus solution.

Date: **Experiment - 05**

TERPIN HYDRATE LICNTUS

Aim: To prepare and submit Terpin Hydrate Linctus

Principle:

Linctus is viscous and sweet liquid preparations containing one or more medicaments used for relief of cough. Such medicaments have expectorant, demulcent and sedative actions. They contain high proportion of syrups and glycerin. Syrups mask the unpleasant taste of drugs and also has soothing effect. Glycerin makes the preparation viscous and possess demulcent action.

Terpin hydrate is used as an expectorant. It is highly soluble in alcohol and slightly soluble in water. Alcohol is used to dissolve terpin hydrate and also acts as preservative, syrup and glycerin acts as vehicles

Procedure:

1. Dissolve required quantity of terpin hydrate in measured quantity of alcohol by stirring in a beaker.
2. Add glycerin and syrup to the beaker containing terpin hydrate solution.
3. Add sufficient water to make the required volume.

Auxiliary label:

DO NOT DILUTE WITH WATER BEFORE USE

Storage: Store in a cool place protected from light.

Direction: Sip, 5ml spoonful and swallow slowly, two times a day undiluted.

Formulation table:

S. No.	Ingredients	Quantity Given	Quantity Taken (factor X quantity given)
1.	Terpin hydrate	50g	
2.	Alcohol	425ml	
3.	Glycerin	400ml	
4.	Syrup	100ml	
5.	Purified water	1000 ml q.s	

Calculations:

Factor = Required quantity/Quantity Given

Label: (Students shall write all aspects of labelling in the space provided below)

TERPIN HYDRATE LICNTUS		
USE: Analgesic, Antipyretic. STORAGE: Store in a cool place protected from light.	A linctus contains:50 g of terpin Dose: 5ml spoonful Name of the institution	Lic.no.______ Mfg. Date:____ Batch no._____ Expiry date ______

Report:

Date: **Experiment - 06**

IODINE THROAT PAINT (MANDL'S PAINT)

Aim: To prepare and submit 20ml of Iodine Throat Paint.

Synonym: Mandl's paint.

Type of product: Throat paint.

Category: Antiseptic and Astringent

Apparatus: Beaker, Glass rod, Measuring Cylinder

Principle: Compound iodine paint or Mandl's paint is a throat paint used in the treatment of pharyngitis, tonsillitis. Paints are liquid preparations intended for application to the mucous membrane or skin. They may contain volatile solvent that evaporates quickly to leave a dry orresinous film of medicaments. Throat paints are viscous liquid preparations used for mouth and throat infections. The commonly used throat paints are Boro glycerin, phenol glycerin, tannic acid glycerin, compound iodine paint. In this preparation iodine acts as antiseptic, potassium iodide dissolves the iodine. Peppermint oil acts as flavouring agent and produce cooling effect. Alcohol is used as a solubilizing agent of the peppermint oil. Glycerin acts as vehicle as it is viscous and adheres to the mucous membranes of the throat for a long time. This preparation should be applied with a fine camel hair brush.

Procedure:

1. Weigh iodine and potassium iodide accurately.
2. Dissolve potassium iodide in water and stir until completely dissolved.
3. Dissolve peppermint oil in alcohol 90% in a small beaker and transfer it into iodine solution.
4. Mix well, add glycerin and mix thoroughly.
5. Transfer to a Measuring Cylinder and make up the volume with glycerin.
6. Transfer the preparation into well closed, colored fluted bottle, attach label and submit.

Direction: Apply with a brush

Label:

NOT TO BE SWALLOWED IN LARGE AMOUNTS

NOT TO BE TAKEN INTERNALLY

SHAKE WELL BEFORE USE

(because some of the volatile oil separates on storage)

Storage: Store in a cool and dry place. Protect from light.

Formulation table:

S.No.	Ingredients	Quantity Given	Quantity taken (factor X quantity given)
1	Iodine	12.5g	
2	Potassium iodide	25.0g	
3	Alcohol 90%	40.0ml	
4	Peppermint oil	4.0ml	
5	Purified water	25.0ml	
6	Glycerin to produce	1000ml	

Calculations:

Factor = required quantity/quantity given

Label:

(Students shall write all aspects of labelling in the space provided below)

IODINE THROAT PAINT (MANDL'S PAINT)		
USE: Antiseptic and Astringent **STORAGE:** Store in a cool and dry place. Protect from light.	A Throat paints. contains: iodine Name of the institution	Lic.no.________ Mfg. Date:____ Batch no.______ Expiry date ____

Report:

CHAPTER - 4

SOLUTIONS-INTRODUCTION

Solutions are homogeneous mixtures composed of two or more substances where one substance (the solute) is uniformly dispersed in another substance (the solvent). In pharmaceuticals and various other fields, solutions serve as common dosage forms for administering medications, delivering nutrients, preparing reagents, and facilitating various chemical processes. They offer advantages such as rapid absorption, precise dosing, and ease of administration.

Classification of Solutions:

Solutions can be classified based on several criteria, including the physical state of the solvent and solute, concentration, and route of administration.

Based on Physical State:

- **Liquid Solutions:** Solutes dissolved in liquid solvents, such as sugar dissolved in water.
- **Gaseous Solutions:** Solutes dissolved in gaseous solvents, such as oxygen dissolved in nitrogen.

Based on Concentration:

- **Dilute Solutions:** Low concentration of solute relative to the solvent, typically expressed in weight per volume (w/v) or volume per volume (v/v) percentages.
- **Concentrated Solutions:** High concentration of solute relative to the solvent.

Based on Route of Administration:

- **Oral Solutions:** Solutions intended for oral administration, such as syrups, elixirs, or oral suspensions.
- **Topical Solutions**: Solutions applied to the skin or mucous membranes, such as antiseptic solutions or eye drops.

- **Injectable Solutions:** Solutions intended for parenteral administration, such as intravenous (IV) infusions or intramuscular (IM) injections.

EXCIPIENTS USED IN SOLUTIONS:

Excipients are additives used in solution formulations to enhance stability, solubility, palatability, and other properties. Common excipients used in solutions include:

Solvents: Water, alcohols, glycols, oils, and organic solvents used as the main liquid component.

Preservatives: Prevent microbial growth and extend shelf-life.

Surfactants: Aid in solubilization and emulsification of insoluble or poorly soluble solutes.

Buffers: Maintain the pH of the solution within a desired range to enhance stability and reduce irritation.

Sweeteners and Flavors: Improve taste and palatability of oral solutions.

Antioxidants: Prevent degradation of active ingredients due to oxidation.

Viscosity Modifiers: Adjust the viscosity of the solution to improve pourability and administration.

Advantages of Solutions:

- Solutions allow for rapid absorption of medications, nutrients, or active ingredients due to their homogeneous nature.
- Solutions facilitate precise dosing, enabling accurate administration of medications or reagents.
- Solutions are typically easy to swallow or apply, making them suitable for patients who have difficulty swallowing tablets or capsules.
- Solutions can accommodate a wide range of solutes and solvents, allowing for versatile formulations tailored to specific requirements.
- Solutions offer flexibility in dosing, as the concentration of the solute can be adjusted to achieve the desired therapeutic effect.

Disadvantages of Solutions:

- Some solutions may be prone to chemical degradation or physical instability over time, requiring special storage conditions or additives to maintain stability.

- Some solutions may have a bitter, unpleasant taste or odor, affecting patient compliance and acceptability.
- Solutions may be bulkier than solid dosage forms, requiring larger containers for storage and transportation.
- Some solutions may have a shorter shelf life compared to solid dosage forms, limiting their storage duration and necessitating frequent replenishment.
- Solutions are susceptible to microbial contamination if not properly formulated, stored, or handled, posing risks to patient safety.

Date: **Experiment - 07**

STRONG AMMONIUM ACETATE SOLUTION

Aim: To prepare, evaluate and submit Strong ammonium acetate solution by pH adjustment method.

Concept: Formation of active ingredient by chemical reaction, to understand the concept of pH adjustment by using indicator solution

Category: Diaphoretic and diuretic.

Dose: 1 to 4 ml.

Apparatus: Conical flask, glass beaker, glass rod, measuring cylinder, dispensing balance

Principle:

Strong ammonium acetate solution is prepared by the chemical reaction method. It is prepared by reaction between glacial acetic acid and ammonium bicarbonate.

$$CH_3COOH + NH_4HCO_3 \longrightarrow CH_3COONH_4 + H_2O + CO_2$$

Glacial acetic acid ***Ammonium bicarbonate*** ***Ammonium acetate***

Carbon dioxide remains in solution giving it a good taste. Ammonia should be used for neutralization of excess of acetic acid. If ammonium bicarbonates used, then it forms a concentrated solution and reaction ceases. To push reaction in forward direction, strong solution of ammonia is added. It also neutralizes the excess acetic acid. Weak solution of ammonium acetate is prepared by a dmixture of one volume of strong solution and seven volumes of distilled water.

The pH is adjusted by using 2 indicators bromothymol blue and thymol blue.

Bromothymol Blue **Neutralization Point** **Thymol Blue**

$$\text{pH 6(yellow)} \longrightarrow \text{pH 7.6(Blue)} \longrightarrow \text{pH 8.0(yellow)} \longrightarrow \text{pH 9.6(Blue)}$$

Procedure:

1. Diluted glacial acetic acid (weight per ml 1.047) with about 350ml of purified water, because ammonium bicarbonate does not dissolve in concentrated solution.
2. To this add ammonium bicarbonate in small quantities at a time with continuous stirring until, whole of it is dissolved.
3. Add sufficient amount of ammonium solution (little at a time) until one drop of the resulting solution diluted with 10 drops of water. Gives a full blue color with one drop of bromothymol blue solution and a full yellow color with one drop of thymol blue solution. It is the neutralization point which lies between pH 7.6 and 8.0.
4. Then add sufficient amount of purified water to produce required volume.

Storage:

Store in a cool and dark place. Store in a lead-free glass container.

Formulation table:

S. No.	Ingredients	Quantity Given	Quantity Taken (factor X quantity given)
1.	Ammonium bicarbonate	470gm	
2.	Glacial acetic acid	453gm	
3.	Strong ammonium solution	q.s	
4.	Purified water q.s	1000ml	

Calculations:

Factor = Required quantity/Quantity Given

Label: (Students shall write all aspects of labelling in the space provided below)

STRONG AMMONIUM ACETATE SOLUTION		
USE: Diaphoretic and diuretic STORAGE: Store in a cool and dark place. Store in a lead-free glass container.	A solution contains: Ammonium bicarbonate Dose:1 to 4 ml. Name of the institution	Lic.no.________ Mfg. Date:_____ Batch no.______ Expiry date ____

Report:

Date: **Experiment - 08**

CRESOL WITH SOAP SOLUTION

Aim: To prepare, evaluate and submit 25ml of Cresol with soap solution IP by micelle formation

Synonym: Lysol solution

Concept: solubility enhancement by micelle formation, saponification reaction

Type of product: Solution for external use (soap making)

Category: Disinfectant

Composition: 50% v/v cresol.

Principle:

Cresol is an active ingredient used as disinfectant. Solubility of cresol in water is 2%v/v, but this preparation contains 50% v/v of cresol. Therefore, the solubility of cresol is increased by using a solubilizing agent, i.e., soap which is formed by in-situ by reaction between vegetable oil and potassium hydroxide. Generally, ortho cresol is used for preparation. Vegetable oils like arachis oil, cotton seed oil, linseed oil or soybean oil or similar oils having saponification value not greater than 205 and an iodine value not less than 100 may be used. Coconut oil and palm kernel oil is not used because of their saponification value and low iodine value.The free fatty acids present in oil react with alkali (potassium or sodium hydroxide) to form soap. The soap acts as a solubilizing agent. Type of soap used also influences the bactericidal power of the solution. Soap forms charged aggregates as ionic micelles. These micelles contain linoleoyl radical which solubilizes cresol giving clear solution. Then required volume is adjusted with purified water.

Procedure:

1. Dissolve potassium hydroxide in required quantity of purified water
2. Add vegetable oil to it.
3. Heat the mixture on water bath till a small portion of mixture dissolves in water without the separation of oily drops.

4. Add cresol to the above mixture and mix thoroughly to get a clear solution.
5. Then add sufficient purified water to make up the volume.

Storage: Store in well closed container protected from light.

Special instruction:

FOR EXTERNAL USE ONLY.

Formulation table:

S. No.	Ingredients	Quantity Given	Quantity Taken (factor X quantity given)
1.	Cresol	500ml	
2.	Arachis oil	180g	
3.	Potassium hydroxide	42g	
4.	Purified water q.s	1000ml	

Calculations:

Factor = Required quantity/Quantity Given

Label: (Students shall write all aspects of labelling in the space provided below)

<table>
<tr><th colspan="3">CRESOL WITH SOAP SOLUTION</th></tr>
<tr>
<td>USE: Disinfectant

STORAGE: Store in well closed container protected from light.</td>
<td>Solution for external use (soap making) contains:50% v/v cresol.

Dose:1 to 4 ml.

Name of the institution</td>
<td>Lic.no.________

Mfg. Date:_____

Batch no.______

Expiry date ____</td>
</tr>
</table>

Report:

Date: **Experiment - 09**

AQUEOUS IODINE SOLUTION (LUGOL'S SOLUTION)

Aim: To prepare and submit Aqueous iodine solution.

Synonym: Lugol's Solution.

Category: Antiseptic.

Dose: 0.3-2 ml when used as a source of iodine.

Storage: preserve in well closed (to prevent its volatilization), light resistant amber coloured (as iodine is light sensitive), narrow mouthed glass fluted containers and store at cool and dark place

Principle:

Iodine: Iodine is active ingredient and is used as an antiseptic.

Potassium iodide: Potassium iodide is used to increase the solubility of iodine. Iodine is very slightly soluble in water, as its solubility in water is 1:2950 but in the presence of potassium iodide it becomes soluble due to the formation of new compounds known as polyiodides i.e., KI, KI.I2, KI.2I2, KI.3I2 KI.nI2, It also prevents the formation of ethyl iodide (might be formed due to reaction of iodine with ethyl alcohol, preventing antiseptic activity of the iodine).In making the preparation potassium iodide may be replaced by sodium iodide.

Alcohol: Alcohol is used as a vehicle. Further,

a) Iodine is freely soluble in alcohol. Hence it reduces the requirement of potassiumiodide.

b) It enhances antiseptic property of the preparation because alcohol itself acts as an antiseptic at higher concentration

c) It acts as permeation enhancer, as alcohol dissolves skin fats thereby increases pore size. Due to increased pore size, rate of absorption of iodine also increases.

d) Due to volatile nature of alcohol, it evaporates quickly after its application leaving behind a film of iodine on skin.

e) The alcohol content in this preparation is 45-48%.

Procedure:

1. Triturate potassium iodide and iodine in glass mortar.
2. Dissolve in sufficient quantity of alcohol (50%v/v).
3. Add required quantity of alcohol to make the volume.
4. Filter through glass wool plugged on glass funnel.

Important – Handling of Iodine:

Iodine stains skin, cloths, porcelain and metals. Therefore, for the preparation/storage of iodine: -

1. Glass pestle mortar should be used instead of porcelain. Similarly, only glass wares should be used and the use of plastic wares should be avoided. Filtration should be done through glass wool only. Filter papers should not be used.
2. Iodine is an oxidizing agent. It oxidizes iron and converts into ferrous iodide. Hence, metal spatula should not be used for handling of iodine. Plastic spoons may be used.
3. Glass (preferably) or plastic container should be used for its storage.
4. If required, iodine stains can be removed by using sodium thiosulphate (hypo) solution

Formulation table:

S. No.	Ingredients	Quantity Given	Quantity Taken (factor X quantity given)
1.	Iodine	20gm	
2.	Potassium iodide	25gm	
3.	Alcohol (50%v/v)	q.s 1000 mL	

Calculations:

Factor = Required quantity/Quantity Given

Label: (Students shall write all aspects of labelling in the space provided below)

AQUEOUS IODINE SOLUTION		
USE: Antiseptic STORAGE: Store in well closed container protected from light and light resistant amber colored bottle.	Solution contains: iodine and 20%alcohol Dose: 0.3-2 ml Name of the institution	Lic.no.________ Mfg. Date:____ Batch no.______ Expiry date ______

Report:

CHAPTER - 5

SUSPENSIONS-INTRODUCTION

Suspensions are bi-phasic liquid dosage forms (or) dispersion Systems, in which the finely divided, insoluble solid particles are suspended (or) dispersed in a liquid. Size of dispersed solids ranges from 0.1 to 1000ml Solid particles constitute Dispersed phase (Internal Phase). Liquid medium constitutes Continuous phase (External (or)Dispersion phase)

Ideal Properties of Suspensions:

- Dispersed particles should not settle rapidly. Even though particles settle down, they should be easily redispersed after shaking.
- Sediment should not form a hard cake; it is difficult to redisperse after shaking.
- Particles should be uniformly distributed throughout the external phase
- Suspensions should have suitable viscosity and also should be palatable (have good taste and odour)
- Suspensions should be physically, chemically and micro – biologically stable.
- It should be free from large particles which spoil its appearance, give a gritty taste to oral preparations and also cause irritation to sensitive tissues when applied externally.
- Suspensions used for external use, should spread easily and leave a film of medicament at the site of application.
- It should be free from large particles which spoil its appearance, give a gritty taste to oral preparations and also cause irritation to sensitive tissues when applied externally

Suspensions Typically Consist of Three Main Components:

Active Pharmaceutical Ingredient (API): The drug substance intended to elicit a therapeutic effect.

Liquid Vehicle (Solvent): The liquid medium in which the drug particles are dispersed. This can be water, oil, or a mixture of both, depending on the solubility and stability requirements of the drug.

Excipients: Inactive ingredients added to the formulation to improve stability, palatability, flow properties, and other characteristics of the suspension. Excipients may include suspending agents, preservatives, flavoring agents, sweeteners, and viscosity modifiers.

Excipient	Function	Examples
Suspending Agent	Prevents settling of particles in the suspension	Methylcellulose, Xanthan Gum, Guar Gum
Preservative	Prevents microbial growth and extends shelf life	Benzyl Alcohol, Methylparaben, Propylparaben
Flavoring Agent	Enhances taste and palatability	Cherry, Raspberry, Orange Flavoring
Sweetening Agent	Adds sweetness to improve taste	Sucrose, Sorbitol, Xylitol
Coloring Agent	Adds color for aesthetic appeal	FD&C Red No. 40, Titanium Dioxide
Viscosity Modifier	Adjusts the thickness or flow properties	Glycerin, Propylene Glycol, Sodium Carboxymethylcellulose
Antioxidant	Prevents oxidation and maintains stability	Ascorbic Acid (Vitamin C), Sodium Metabisulfite
pH Adjuster	Controls pH to optimize stability and solubility	Citric Acid, Sodium Citrate, Sodium Hydroxide
Wetting Agent	Improves wetting and dispersion of particles	Polysorbate 80, Tween 80, Sodium Lauryl Sulfate
Dispersing Agent	Promotes even distribution of particles in the liquid	Sodium Carboxymethylcellulose, Tween 80

Excipients used in preparation of suspensions:

General Method for preparation of Suspensions:

- Carefully tare the container.
- Finely powder the solid ingredients.
- Mix the insoluble powders in a mortar and add enough vehicle to make a smooth cream.
- Add more quantity of vehicle to make it pourable.
- Examine the Suspension carefully and if contains foreign particles, strain, Through a muslin cloth into a tared container.
- Rinse the mortar and pestle with successive volume of the vehicle until they are quite clean.
- Transfer the rinsings to the bottle Add any liquid ingredient.
- Add more vehicle to produce the required volume and mix thoroughly by shaking the bottle

CONTAINERS AND STORAGE:

Suspensions should be packed in containers that have adequate air space above liquid to permit shaking oral suspensions should be packed in wide mouthed bottles to permit prompt removal of suspension These Should be stored in cool place but not in refrigerator. Freezing at low temperature leads to aggregation of suspended particles.

LABELLING:

Must be labelled with a secondary label "SHAKE WELL BEFORE USE" In case of dry suspensions, amount of vehicle to be mixed may be implicated clearly on label.

FLOCCULATED AND DE- FLOCCULATED SUSPENSIONS:

Flocculated Suspensions	De flocculated Suspensions
1) Individual particles of Suspended phase contact with one another and form a loose network like structure (floccules (or) aggregates)	1)Each Suspended particle exists as Separate entity, hard cake is formed which is very difficult to redisperse to get a homogenous Suspension after shaking.
2) Rate of sedimentation is fast (high) due to density of floccules is very high	2)Rate of sedimentation is low due to less density of individual particles
3)Sediment is loosely packed	3)Sediment formed is hard compact cake
4)loosely packed sediment can be easily re-dispersed by moderate shaking	4)Hard cake is difficult to re-disperse by moderate shaking
5) Bio-availability in flocculated Suspension is low (slow)	5)Bio-availability in de-flocculated Suspension is high (fast)
6)These have non – elegant appearance, Because floccules stick to the walls of container	6)These are elegant in appearance, after sedimentation particles will not stick to walls of container
7) Sediment volume is high	7) Sediment volume is small
8)Supernatant liquid becomes clear because floccules settle down rapidly	8) Supernatant liquid became (or) remains cloudy for long time,

Date:

Experiment - 10

CALAMINE LOTION IP

Aim: To prepare and submit 20ml of calamine lotion.

Type of product: suspension for external preparation containing indiffusible solids.

Category: Skin protective.

Composition: Calamine 15% w/v; zinc oxide 5% w/v.

Apparatus: Mortar and pestle, pipette, measuring cylinder, beakers, glass rod.

Principle: Calamine and zinc oxide is used as astringent, soothing and protecting agent. Bentonite is suspending agent. Sodium citrate is used as deflocculating and chelating agent. It also acts as buffer. Liquefied phenol is used as antiseptic and preservative. Calamine lotion is a suspension of indiffusible solids like calamine and zinc oxide. Calamine is obtained from mineral sources and consists of 98% zinc oxide with small amounts of ferric oxide. The characteristic pink colour of the calamine and its preparation is due to the presence of ferric oxide only. Zinc oxide is added to maintain this distinctive colour (similar to skin) of the preparation. The preparation will have dark reddish colour, if calamine alone is used bentonite is incorporated to uniformly diffuse calamine and zinc oxide.

Bentonite is a naturally occurring colloidal hydrated Aluminium silicate. It absorbs water (12 times of its weight), swells up and forms magma, making the preparation highly viscous which is difficult to pour from the container. Sodium citrate causes partial deflocculation of calamine and zinc oxide, and reduces the viscosity of the preparation to a pourable consistency.Sodium citrate also chelates with free iron of the ferric oxide and prevents discoloration of the preparation. It also maintains the pH of the preparation. Glycerin keeps the skin moist for longer time. It also gives cooling and soothing effect to the skin.

Procedure:

1. Triturate the calamine, zinc oxide and bentonite with a solution of the sodium citrate in purified water.
2. Add the liquefied phenol, glycerin and sufficient rose water to produce final quantity.

Storage: It is stored in well closed, narrow mouthed plastic screw capped fluted bottles incool place

Special instruction:

1. FOR EXTERNAL USE ONLY.
2. SHAKE WELL BEFORE USE.

Formulation table:

S. No.	Ingredients	Quantity Given	Quantity taken (factor X quantity given)
1	Zinc oxide	50gm	
2	Calamine	150gm	
3	Sodium citrate	5gm	
4	Bentonite	30gm	
5	Liquid phenol	5ml	
6	Glycerol	50ml	
7	Rose water q.s	1000ml	

Calculations:

Factor = required quantity/quantity given

Label: (Students shall write all aspects of labelling in the space provided below)

CALAMINE LOTION IP		
USE: Skin protective STORAGE: stored in well closed, narrow mouthed plastic screw capped fluted bottles incool place	Lotion contains: Calamine 15% w/v; zinc oxide 5% w/v Name of the institution	Lic.no.________ Mfg. Date:____ Batch no.______ Expiry date ______

Report:

Date: **Experiment -11**

MAGNESIUM HYDROXIDE MIXTURE

Aim: To prepare and submit 20ml of magnesium hydroxide suspension.

Synonym: Milk of magnesia, Cream of magnesia.

Type of product: Oral suspension containing diffusible solids.

Category: Antacid, laxative.

Composition: Magnesium hydroxide 7.9% w/v.

Dose: Antacid-5-10ml, laxative 15-30ml.

Principle: Magnesium hydroxide mixture is an aqueous colloidal dispersion of magnesium hydroxide. It is prepared by two methods.

- **Precipitation method**: Sodium hydroxide reacts with magnesium sulphate to form a precipitate of magnesium hydroxide and sodium sulphate. The precipitate obtained will sediment quickly.

$$MgSO_4 + 2\ NaOH \longrightarrow Mg(OH)_2 \downarrow + Na_2SO_4$$

- **Hydration method:** Magnesium hydroxide is prepared by the hydration of light magnesium oxide. The product is highly viscous and unpourable

$$MgO + H_2O \xrightarrow{\text{Heat}} Mg(OH)_2 \downarrow$$

Hence magnesium hydroxide is prepared by two reactions. The product obtained from combination of two reactions will have optimum viscosity with minimum settling. During the preparation, magnesium hydroxide should be free from sulphates. The precipitate is washed with pure water on filter paper until it is free from sulphates. After washing the precipitate,the filtrate is tested for sulphates using barium chloride reagent. Chloroform water is used as preservative.

Procedure:

1. Dissolve sodium hydroxide in purified water. Add this solution to a mortar containing magnesium sulphate and mix to form a smooth dispersion and add sufficient water to produce half volume. Transfer the contents in to beaker.

2. Prepare solution in another beaker by dissolving the light magnesium oxide in purified water. Add the content of first beaker to second beaker i.e. to magnesium oxide solution. Keep the dispersion aside.
3. Decant the clear liquid.
4. **Test for sulphates:** To 5ml of decanted solution add 1ml of 2M hydrochloric acid and 1ml of 6.1% w/v barium chloride solution. A white precipitate indicates the presence of sulphates.
5. Wash the precipitate until the washings gives only slight reaction for sulphates.
6. Mix the washed precipitate with small quantity of purified water, add double strength chloroform water and add sufficient purified water to make up the required volume.
7. Pack it in a clean, dry bottle and label it.

Special instruction:

SHAKE WELL BEFORE USE.

Storage: Store in a well closed container in a cool and dry place.

S. No.	Ingredients	Quantity Given	Quantity Taken (factor X quantity given)
1	Magnesium sulphate	47.5gm	
2	Sodium hydroxide	15gm	
3	Light magnesium oxide	52.5gm	
4	Chloroform water (double strength)	2.5ml	
5	Purified water q.s	1000ml	

Calculations:

Factor = Required Quantity/Quantity Given

Label: (Students shall write all aspects of labelling in the space provided below)

MAGNESIUM HYDROXIDE MIXTURE		
USE: Antacid, laxative STORAGE: Store in a well closed container in a cool and dry place.	Mixture contains: Magnesium hydroxide 7.9% w/v. Dose: Antacid-5-10ml, laxative 15-30ml Name of the institution	Lic.no.________ Mfg. Date:_____ Batch no.______ Expiry date ____

Report:

Date: **Experiment -12**

ALUMINIUM HYDROXIDE GEL

Aim: To prepare and submit 25 ml of Aluminum hydroxide gel IP

Type of product: Oral suspension

Category: Antacid

Composition: Hydrated Aluminum Oxide -3.5% w/w

Dose: 8-10ml

Apparatus: Water bath (copper vessel and wire gauze), beaker, glass rod, Magnetic stirrer.

Principle: Gels are the biphasic semi-solid dosage from. These are viscous aqueous suspension contains precipitate of inorganic compounds having particle size closer to colloidal range prepared without addition of any suspending agent. These are also termed as shake preparations. Aluminium hydroxide gel is aqueous suspension of Aluminium hydroxide and the hydrated Aluminium oxide produced from ammonium alum. Peppermint oil acts as aflavouring agent. Sodium benzoate acts as a preservative. Purified water acts as a vehicle.

Procedure:

1. Divide the total amount of water required into two equal portions.
2. Heat one portion to make hot water.
3. Divide the hot water into two portions and dissolve sodium carbonate and ammonium alum separately with constant stirring.
4. Dilute the resulting solutionwith some portion of cold water, precipitate will be formed at this stage.
5. Collect and wash the precipitates and suspend in purified water containing peppermint oil and sodium benzoate.
6. Stir the resulting gel to get a homogenous mass on a magnetic stirrer and dispense.

Storage: Store in a well closed container in a cool and dry place.

Special Instructions:

SHAKE WELL BEFORE USE.

FREEZING MUST BE AVOIDED.

Formulation Table:

S. No.	Ingredients	Quantity Given	Quantity Taken (factor X quantity given
1.	Ammonium alum	40 g	
2.	Sodium carbonate	50 g	
3.	Peppermint oil	0.1 ml	
4.	Sodium benzoate	0.1 g	
5.	Purified water q.s	100 ml	

Calculations:

Factor = Required Quantity/Quantity Given

Label: (Students shall write all aspects of labelling in the space provided below)

ALUMINIUM HYDROXIDE GEL		
USE: counter irritant STORAGE: Store in a tightly closed, narrow mouthed, plastic screw capped fluted colored bottles, and in cool place.	Mixture contains: Hydrated Aluminum Oxide -3.5% w/w Dose: 8-10ml Name of the institution	Lic.no.________ Mfg. Date:_____ Batch no._______ Expiry date ____

Report:

CHAPTER - 6

EMULSIONS – INTRODUCTION

Emulsions are a type of colloidal dispersion consisting of two immiscible liquids, typically oil and water, stabilized by an emulsifying agent. In an emulsion, tiny droplets of one liquid (the dispersed phase) are dispersed throughout the other liquid (the continuous phase), forming a homogeneous mixture. Emulsions are commonly encountered in various industries, including food, cosmetics, pharmaceuticals, and paints, where they serve essential functions and offer unique properties.

Emulsions are classified based on the nature of the dispersed and continuous phases:

Oil-in-Water (O/W) Emulsions: In these emulsions, oil droplets are dispersed within a continuous phase of water. O/W emulsions are commonly used in applications where water is the predominant phase, such as skincare products, salad dressings, and certain pharmaceutical formulations.

Water-in-Oil (W/O) Emulsions: Here, water droplets are dispersed within a continuous phase of oil. W/O emulsions are utilized in situations where oil is the dominant phase, such as certain types of creams, lotions, and industrial lubricants.

Emulsions are stabilized by emulsifiers or surfactants, which lower the interfacial tension between the two immiscible liquids, preventing the droplets from coalescing and forming separate layers. Emulsifiers have a hydrophilic (water-attracting) portion that interacts with the aqueous phase and a hydrophobic (oil-attracting) portion that interacts with the oil phase, allowing them to effectively stabilize the interface between the two phases.

Emulsions Offer Several Advantages in Various Applications:

Improved Stability: Emulsions can enhance the stability of certain formulations by preventing phase separation and sedimentation of particles.

Texture and Sensory Properties: Emulsions can provide desirable textures, appearances, and sensory experiences in products like creams, lotions, and food products.

Enhanced Solubility and Bioavailability: Emulsions can improve the solubility and bioavailability of poorly soluble substances, making them valuable in pharmaceutical formulations and food fortification.

Controlled Release: Emulsions can be engineered to control the release of active ingredients, enabling sustained or targeted delivery for pharmaceuticals, agrochemicals, and personal care products.

Versatility: Emulsions are versatile and can be tailored to meet specific requirements by adjusting the composition, stability, and properties of the formulation.

Special Type of Emulsions (Depending on the Globule Size):

Emulsions can be classified into different types based on the size of the dispersed droplets. The size of the droplets influences various properties of the emulsion, including stability, appearance, texture, and functionality. Here are some special types of emulsions based on globule size:

Macroemulsions: These are conventional emulsions with relatively large droplet sizes, typically in the range of 0.1 to 100 micrometers (μm) in diameter. Macroemulsions are commonly used in food products, cosmetics, pharmaceuticals, and industrial applications. They are often opaque and have a creamy or milky appearance.

Microemulsions: Microemulsions are thermodynamically stable, transparent or translucent emulsions with very small droplet sizes, typically less than 100 nanometers (nm) in diameter. These emulsions have a clear appearance and can be formed spontaneously without the need for high shear mixing or extensive emulsifier concentrations. Microemulsions are utilized in various applications, including drug delivery systems, enhanced oil recovery, and nanotechnology.

RATIO OF PRIMARY EMULSION:

Type of Emulsion	Primary Phase	Secondary Phase	Ratio (Primary: Secondary)
Oil-in-Water (O/W)	Oil	Water	Typically, 1:3 to 1:9
Water-in-Oil (W/O)	Water	Oil	Typically, 3:1 to 9:1

Formulation of Emulsions:

Emulsions can be formulated for various applications, including cosmetics, pharmaceuticals, food products, and industrial uses. The specific formulation depends on factors such as the desired properties of the emulsion, the intended application, and the characteristics of the ingredients used. Here are general guidelines for formulating emulsions:

Select Ingredients: Choose appropriate oils, water, emulsifiers, thickeners, preservatives, and other additives based on the desired characteristics and application of the emulsion. Consider factors such as solubility, stability, compatibility, and safety of the ingredients.

Phase Ratio: Determine the ratio of the oil phase to the water phase based on the type of emulsion (O/W or W/O) and the desired consistency and texture of the final product. Typically, O/W emulsions have a higher water phase ratio, while W/O emulsions have a higher oil phase ratio.

Emulsifier Selection: Select an appropriate emulsifier or combination of emulsifiers to stabilize the emulsion and prevent phase separation. Emulsifiers can be hydrophilic (water-loving), lipophilic (oil-loving), or amphiphilic (both water- and oil-loving), depending on the nature of the emulsion and the desired properties.

Emulsification Technique: Use suitable emulsification techniques such as high shear mixing, homogenization, or sonication to achieve fine droplet size and uniform distribution of the dispersed phase within the continuous phase. The emulsification process should be gentle enough to avoid destabilizing the emulsion while ensuring thorough mixing and dispersion of ingredients.

Thickening and Stabilization: Incorporate thickeners, stabilizers, or viscosity modifiers to control the rheology and stability of the emulsion. These additives help prevent creaming, sedimentation, or coalescence of droplets over time, ensuring long-term stability and consistency of the product.

pH Adjustment: Adjust the pH of the emulsion to optimize stability, solubility, and compatibility with other ingredients. pH adjustment may be necessary to maintain the desired texture, appearance, and skin compatibility of cosmetic or pharmaceutical emulsions.

Preservation: Incorporate preservatives or antimicrobial agents to prevent microbial growth and ensure the microbiological safety and shelf life of the emulsion. Choose preservatives that are effective against a broad spectrum of microorganisms while remaining compatible with other ingredients and regulatory requirements.

Quality Control: Conduct thorough quality control tests, including visual inspection, stability testing, pH measurement, viscosity determination, and microbial testing, to ensure the safety, efficacy, and consistency of the emulsion formulation.

Method of Preparation:

Dry Gum Method:

In the dry gum method, the emulsifier (usually a gum or a combination of gums) is first mixed with the oil phase before adding the water phase.

Steps:

1. Dissolve the emulsifier (e.g., gum Arabic, acacia gum, or tragacanth) in the oil phase at room temperature. This forms a thickened oil phase.
2. Slowly add the water phase to the oil phase while continuously stirring or mixing vigorously. The emulsifier helps stabilize the oil droplets in the water phase.
3. Continue mixing until a stable emulsion is formed. Optionally, further homogenize or shear the emulsion to reduce droplet size and improve stability.

Wet Gum Method:

1. In the wet gum method, the emulsifier is first dissolved in the water phase before adding the oil phase.
2. Steps:
3. Dissolve the emulsifier (e.g., gum Arabic, acacia gum, or xanthan gum) in the water phase at room temperature. This forms a thickened water phase.
4. Slowly add the oil phase to the water phase while continuously stirring or mixing vigorously. The emulsifier helps stabilize the water droplets in the oil phase.
5. Continue mixing until a stable emulsion is formed. Optionally, further homogenize or shear the emulsion to reduce droplet size and improve stability.

Bottle Method:

The bottle method is a simple and convenient technique for preparing small-scale emulsions using a bottle or vial.

Steps:

1. Place the oil phase and water phase (each containing the appropriate ingredients) into separate containers.
2. Add the oil phase to a clean, dry bottle or vial, followed by the water phase.
3. Securely close the bottle or vial and shake vigorously to mix the two phases. The emulsifier helps stabilize the emulsion by reducing interfacial tension between the oil and water phases.
4. Continue shaking until a stable emulsion is formed. Optionally, further homogenize or shear the emulsion using additional mixing techniques.

Advantages:

- Prevents separation of immiscible components.
- Improves solubility of hydrophobic compounds.
- Can be tailored for diverse applications.
- Provides desirable textures and appearances.
- Enables targeted or sustained release of active ingredients.
- Simple to formulate and process.
- Enhances absorption of nutrients and bioactive compounds.

Disadvantages:

- Susceptible to phase separation or creaming over time.
- Requires careful selection of emulsifiers and stabilizers.
- Vulnerable to temperature changes and shear forces.
- May degrade or spoil if not properly preserved.
- Some individuals may have allergic reactions to emulsion components.
- High-energy methods required for production may increase costs.

Date:

Experiment - 13

TURPENTINE LINIMENT

Aim: To prepare, evaluate, and submit 10ml of Turpentine liniment.

Category: Counter irritant

Apparatus: Measuring cylinder, pipette, dropper, bottle

Principle:

Liniments are liquid or semisolid preparations meant for application to the unbroken skin with friction. They may be solutions of soap or emulsions. The oil or soap base provides ease of application and massage. Liniments usually contain counter irritants like camphor or turpentine or methyl salicylate.

Turpentine oil acts as counter-irritant and rubefacient. It is volatile oil and does not contain any free fatty acid. It cannot form soap with alkaline substances. It is not miscible with water. Camphor is soluble in turpentine oil. Therefore, soft soap (monovalent) is used to prepare an o/w emulsion of camphorated turpentine oil. Soft soap is required as emulsifying agent. Camphor is used as counter irritant.

Procedure:

1. Dissolve camphor in turpentine oil.
2. Mix soft soap with 100ml of purified water.
3. Add camphor solution to the soap solution gradually with trituration in a mortar and pestle until a thick creamy emulsion is formed.

Use: Turpentine liniment is used as counter irritant and rubefacient, especially by the patients suffering from arthralgia (joint pains), myalgia (muscular pain), fibrositis (ligamental pain) and sprain

Storage: Store in a tightly closed, narrow mouthed, plastic screw capped fluted coloured bottles, and in cool place.

Direction: To be applied on the skin with friction.

Special Instruction:

FOR EXTERNAL USE ONLY

SHAKE WELL BEFORE USE

NOT TO BE APPLIED ON BROKEN SKIN

Formulation Table:

S. No.	Ingredients	Quantity Given	Quantity Taken (factor X quantity given
1.	Soft soap	90gm	
2.	Camphor	50gm	
3.	Turpentine oil	650ml	
4.	Purified water	q.s. 1000ml	

Calculations:

Factor = Required Quantity/Quantity Given

Label: (Students shall write all aspects of labelling in the space provided below)

TURPENTINE LINIMENT		
USE:Antacid, laxative STORAGE: Store in a well closed container in a cool and dry place.	Liniment contains: Turpentine oil Dose: 8-10ml Name of the institution	Lic.no.________ Mfg. Date:____ Batch no.______ Expiry date _______

Report:

Date: **Experiment – 14**

LIQUID PARAFFIN EMULSION

Aim: To prepare and submit liquid paraffin emulsion.

Type of product: O/W emulsion.

Category: Laxative.

Composition: Each 10 ml of emulsion contains 5 ml of liquid paraffin.

Dose: 8-30 ml

Apparatus: Mortar and pestle, dropper, measuring cylinder, pipette, beakers, glass rod andplastic funnel.

Principle:

Emulsion is a biphasic system containing two immiscible liquids i.e. one of the liquids is intimately dispersed as tiny globules in another liquid. The disperse liquid is called internal phase or dispersed phase and other liquid called as external phase or continuous phase. The emulsion is stabilized by using an emulgent. Liquid paraffin emulsion is an oral laxative product and it is administered to the patient in the form of an o/w oral emulsion.

The emulsion is prepared as o/w emulsion by using acacia as emulsifying agent. In preparing emulsion first a primary emulsion is prepared with a set ration of O: W: G (3:2:1). This set ratio is used to mineral oils to prepare primary emulsion. In this emulsion tragacanth gum is used as secondary emulgent (a secondary emulgent is used along with the primary emulgent Acacia in preparing emulsion). Tragacanth acts as secondary emulgent to increases the viscosity of external phase, prevents creaming and also increases the stability of an emulsion. These preparations contain glycerin which acts as a demulcent i.e., it exerts a soothing or protective influence on the gastro intestinal tract. This emulsion is prepared by wet gum method.

Procedure:

1. Take required quantity of acacia and tragacanth in a clean, dry mortar.
2. Add water and prepare smooth mucilage without any lumps.
3. Take liquid paraffin in a clean dry beaker. Dissolve vanillin in it.

4. Add the only solution in small quantities to the mucilage and triturate briskly to prepare a white viscous primary emulsion.
5. Add glycerin to the primary emulsion and mix it. Add chloroform and mix it.
6. Dissolve sodium benzoate in small quantity of water and dilute the primary emulsion and make up the volume.
7. Pack it in a suitable container and label it.

Storage: Store in a cool and dark place.

Special instruction: SHAKE WELL BEFORE USE.

Formulation table:

S. No.	Ingredients	Quantity Given	Quantity Taken (factor X quantity given)
1.	Liquid paraffin	50ml	
2.	Acacia	q.s	
3.	Tragacanth	0.5gm	
4.	Sodium benzoate	0.5gm	
5.	Vanillin	0.05gm	
6.	Glycerin	12.5ml	
7.	Chloroform	0.25ml	
8.	Purified water q.s	100ml	

Calculations:

Factor = Required Quantity/Quantity Given

Label: (Students shall write all aspects of labelling in the space provided below)

LIQUID PARAFFIN EMULSION		
USE: Laxative. STORAGE: Store in a well closed container in a cool and dry place.	An Emulsion**, each** 10 ml of emulsion contains 5 ml of liquid paraffin. Dose: 8-30ml Name of the institution	Lic.no.________ Mfg. Date:_____ Batch no.______ Expiry date ____

Report:

CHAPTER - 7

POWDERS AND GRANULE'S INTRODUCTION

Powders and granules are solid dosage forms used in pharmaceuticals, food, cosmetics, agriculture, and various industrial applications. They consist of finely divided particles of active ingredients, excipients, or additives, which may be dry or granulated to improve handling, flow properties, and uniformity.

POWDERS:

Definition: Powders are solid dosage forms composed of finely divided particles of one or more substances. They can be single-component powders (containing only one substance) or mixture powders (containing multiple substances).

TYPES OF POWDERS:

Bulk Powders: Loose, unconfined powders used for compounding, blending, or filling capsules.

Divided Powders: Single-dose packets containing a specific quantity of a powdered medication for oral or topical administration.

Effervescent Powders: Powders containing effervescent agents that release carbon dioxide when dissolved in water, used for preparing fizzy beverages or effervescent tablets.

PREPARATION:

Powders are typically prepared by grinding, milling, or comminution of solid materials into fine particles. They may also be produced by precipitation, spray drying, or lyophilization for certain applications.

Handling and Administration: Powders are often administered orally, topically, or via inhalation. They may be encapsulated in gelatin capsules, mixed with liquids or semi-solids for oral administration, or applied directly to the skin or mucous membranes.

GRANULES:

Definition: Granules are agglomerates of fine powder particles bound together by cohesive forces to form larger, free-flowing particles with improved flow and handling properties.

TYPES OF GRANULES:

Spherical Granules: Uniformly shaped granules produced by extrusion, spheronization, or pelletization.

Irregular Granules: Non-uniformly shaped granules formed by compaction, crushing, or granulation of powders.

PREPARATION:

The preparation of granules involves agglomerating fine powder particles to form larger, free-flowing particles with improved handling and processing properties. Granules are commonly used in pharmaceuticals, food processing, and other industries.

WET GRANULATION:

Blending: Blend the active pharmaceutical ingredient (API), excipients, and other powder ingredients to form a homogeneous mixture.

Granulation Liquid Preparation: Prepare a granulating liquid, typically consisting of water or a solvent, along with binders, wetting agents, and sometimes disintegrants or lubricants.

Granulation Process: Add the granulating liquid to the powder mixture while mixing, either in a high-shear mixer, a fluid bed granulator, or a planetary mixer. The liquid wets the powder particles, causing them to bind together and form granules.

Drying: Dry the wet granules using a fluid bed dryer, tray dryer, or oven to remove excess moisture and stabilize the granule structure.

Sizing and Screening: Optionally, screen or sieve the dried granules to achieve the desired particle size distribution.

DRY GRANULATION (ROLLER COMPACTION):

a) **Blending:** Blend the powder ingredients as in wet granulation.

b) **Compaction:** Feed the powder blend between two counter-rotating rollers in a roller compactor. The rollers compress the powder into a ribbon or sheet, causing particle bonding and densification.

c) Milling: Mill the compacted ribbon or sheet into granules using a mill or granulator. The milling process breaks up the compacted material into granules of the desired size.

d) Sizing and Screening: Optionally, screen or sieve the milled granules to achieve the desired particle size distribution.

FLUID BED GRANULATION:

a) Powder Suspension: Fluidize the powder mixture in a fluid bed granulator using a stream of air or inert gas. The fluidization promotes mixing and particle movement.

b) Spray Granulation: Spray a granulating liquid onto the fluidized powder bed using atomizing nozzles. The liquid wets the powder particles, causing them to agglomerate and form granules.

c) Drying: Dry the wet granules in the fluid bed granulator or transfer them to a separate dryer to remove moisture and stabilize the granule structure.

d) Sizing and Screening: Optionally, screen or sieve the dried granules to achieve the desired particle size distribution.

SPRAY GRANULATION:

a) Atomization: Atomize a liquid feed containing the API, binders, and other additives using a spray nozzle or atomizer.

b) Droplet Drying: Allow the atomized droplets to dry in a drying chamber or fluid bed dryer, where solvent evaporation leads to the formation of granules.

c) Sizing and Screening: Optionally, screen or sieve the dried granules to achieve the desired particle size distribution.

Advantages:

Granules offer several advantages over powders, including improved flowability, reduced dustiness, better compressibility, and enhanced uniformity of drug distribution in solid dosage forms such as tablets and capsules.

Powders and granules are versatile dosage forms widely used in various industries for their ease of handling, flexibility in formulation, and suitability for a wide range of applications. They play a critical role in drug delivery, product manufacturing, and material processing, contributing to advancements in healthcare, nutrition, and technology.

Dispensing: Weigh the required quantity of granules and transfer them into a narrow-mouthed bottle tightlyclosed with a colored plastic screw cap.

Direction: Add two spoonsful of granules, to a glass of water by stirring and drink the solution.

Storage: Store in a dry place and protect from light.

Date: Experiment - 15

ORAL REHYDRATION SALT

Aim: To prepare and submit10 g of oral rehydration salt.

Synonym: ORS powder

Category: fluid and electrolyte replacement in diarrhoea.

Apparatus: sieves, paper sheets, spatula

Principle: This formula is official in IP &BP as WHO-ORS citrate. The ORS formula is choice of treatment to treat water loss during diarrhoea. The ORS enhances the absorption of water and electrolytes. Glucose is absorbed in the small intestine, as in parts of nephron through transport carriers, coupled with sodium ions. Thus, increased glucose increases intestinal absorption of sodium and passive re-absorption of water, therefore sodium chloride,potassium chloride and glucose of frequently used components of ORS. The palatability of powder is attributed to the presence of glucose and it is further built by the addition of citrates or fruit flavors. However, the concentration of glucose can cause osmotic diarrhoea and also aggravate existing diarrhoea. Therefore, the ORS should be isotonic to body fluids. The glucose: sodium ions molar ratio should be 1:1 or 2:1 the low sodium content is suggested to paediatrics. The ORS also contain alkalizing agents such as sodium bicarbonate to counteract acidosis. However, the hygroscopic natures of Sodium bicarbonate affect the storage stability of ORS formula.

Procedure:

1. Sieve the powders using sieve number 60.
2. All ingredients were weighed and mixed in the increasing order of their weights.

Direction: Add the contents of ORS packet into a clean container. Add the correct amount of freshly boiled and cooled water. Do not add ORS to milk, soup, fruit juices or soft drinks

Label:

NOT FOR INJECTION

Storage: Store in well closed container in a cool and dry place.

Formulation table:

S. No	Ingredients	Quantity Given	Quantity Taken (factor X quantity given)
1.	Sodium chloride	3.5g	
2.	Potassium chloride	1.5 g	
3.	Sodium citrate	2.9 g	
4.	Anhydrous glucose	20g	

Calculations:

Factor = Required Quantity/Quantity Given

Label: (Students shall write all aspects of labelling in the space provided below)

ORAL REHYDRATION SALT		
USE: fluid and electrolyte replacement in diarrhoea STORAGE: Store in a well closed container in a cool and dry place.	ORS powder which contains electrolytes. Name of the institution	Lic.no.________ Mfg. Date:____ Batch no.______ Expiry date ______

Report:

Date: **Experiment - 16**

EFFERVESCENT SODIUM PHOSPHATE GRANULES USP

Aim: To prepare and submit 20 gm of the sodium phosphate effervescent granules.

Requirements: Mortar and pestle, porcelain dish, sieves, hot air oven

Category: saline purgative and mild diuretic

Dose: 3-25gm equals to 0.6-5.0g of dried sodium phosphate.

Apparatus: Porcelain dish, sieve, glass rod, a sheet of paper, a sheet of butter paper, spatula.

Principle:

Sodium phosphate effervescent granules are used as a cathartic. This is prepared by heat method. During heating, if the dish is sufficiently hot, water liberates from crystals of citric acid. If heating of the dish is delayed, the powder gets slowly heated up and the liberated water of crystallization evaporate slowly. As a result, sufficient water will not be available to make a coherent mass. The water needed for granulation also comes from the following reactions.

In the formula, sodium phosphate is responsible for cathartic action. The other ingredients undergo the following reactions, when placed in water to produce effervescence.

$$C_6H_8O_7.H_2O \longrightarrow C_6H_5\,Na_3O_7 + 3H_2O + 3CO_2\uparrow$$

Citric acid *water carbon dioxide*

$$C_4H_6O_6 + 2\,NaHCO_3 \longrightarrow Na_2C_4H_4O_6 + 2H_2O + 2CO_2\uparrow$$

Tartaric acid sodium bicarbonate sodium tartarate

Each 10 gm of the powder contains 2 gm of sodium phosphate. The sum of the ingredients is more than 1000 gm, because there is a certain loss of weight of a preparation during granulation because of

A) Evaporation of water from the damp mixture.

B) Loss of carbon dioxide due to its release.

These losses constitute approximately one – seventh of the weight of powder used and must be taken into consideration while calculating the quantity of granules to be prepared.one must be sure that the ingredients are dry.

Procedure:

1. Powder citric acid and mix intimately with dried sodium phosphate and tartaric acid,to make a uniform powder mixture sodium bicarbonate is not added at this stage as it may react with acids
2. Add sodium bicarbonate to the above mixture and mix gently to make the product effervescent.
3. The final powder mixture is placed on a plate of glass or in a suitable dish previously heated on a water bath (so as to evolve one mole of water of crystallization of citric acid)
4. Stir the mixture with help of spatula constantly till it becomes damp (damp mass isformed due to water formed in the reaction)
5. Pass damp mass through sieve no.6 to obtain granules
6. Dry the granules at a temperature not exceeding 55^0c to avoid complete neutralization otherwise the final product will not be effervescent
7. Pass the dried granules through appropriate sieve to break the larger granules touniform size.
8. Pack the dried uniform sized granules in a wide mouthed bottle

Storage:

Keep in air tight container in a cool place.

Direction:

Dissolve two spoonsful of the powder in a glass of water and drink the solution after the effervescence ceases.

Formulation table:

S. No	Ingredients	Quantity Given	Quantity Taken (factor X quantity given)
1.	Sodium phosphate	200gm	
2.	Sodium bicarbonate	477gm	
3.	Tartaric acid	252gm	
4.	Citric acid	162gm	

Calculations

Factor = Required Quantity/Quantity Given

Label: (Students shall write all aspects of labelling in the space provided below)

EFFERVESCENT SODIUM PHOSPHATEGRANULES USP		
USE: saline purgative and mild diuretic STORAGE: Keep in air tight container in a cool place.	The effervescent granules which Dose is 3-25gm equals to 0.6-5.0g of dried sodium phosphate. Name of the institution	Lic.no.________ Mfg. Date:_____ Batch no._______ Expiry date _____

Report:

Date: **Experiment -17**

ZINC OXIDE DUSTING POWDER BPC

Aim: To prepare and submit 10 g of zinc oxide dusting powder.

Type of product: Dusting powder

Category: Astringent, Antiseptic

Apparatus: Mortar and pestle, spatula, a white paper sheet, a sheet of butter paper or a sifter top container.

Principle: This is a medicated dusting powder containing eutectic and volatile substances. Zinc oxide is an astringent; menthol and camphor are antiseptic and when they evaporate, produce a cooling effect on the inflamed area. Magnesium stearate and talc imparts slip property and provides covering. Talc is obtained from natural sources and before mixing with other ingredients it should be sterilized by dry heat sterilization. The formula contains menthol and camphor as eutectic substances and this can be mixed after trituration with other solids. Both talc and zinc oxide, by virtue of their surface area, have capacity of adsorption. One eutectic substance should be triturated with one of the solid.

Procedure:

1. Pulverize camphor and weigh required amount of camphor and mix with half of the weight of talc.
2. Separately weigh required amount of menthol, triturate it and add remaining amount of talc.
3. Mix both the powder mixtures by spatulation.
4. Add zinc oxide and magnesium stearate to get a uniform powder mixture.
5. Pack the powder mixture in a paper packet lined with butter paper (double wrapping is required because camphor and menthol are volatile in nature)

Direction:

FOR EXTERNAL USE ONLY

NOT TO BE APPLIED TO RAW OR WEEPING SURFACES

Label: Keep out of reach of infants

Storage:

Keep the powders in a well closed air tight container. Store in cool place

Formulation table:

S. No	Ingredients	Quantity Given	Quantity Taken (factor X quantity given)
1.	Zinc oxide	20 g	
2.	Menthol	0.25 g	
3.	Camphor	0.5 g	
4.	Magnesium stearate	2 g	
5.	Talc	77.5 g	

Calculations

Factor = Required Quantity/Quantity Given

Label: (Students shall write all aspects of labelling in the space provided below)

ZINC OXIDE DUSTING POWDER BPC		
USE: Astringent, Antiseptic STORAGE: Keep the powders in a well closed air tight container. Store in cool place	A dusting powder which contains 20g of zinc oxide Name of the institution	Lic.no.________ Mfg. Date:_____ Batch no.______ Expiry date ________

Report:

Date:

Experiment - 18

DIVIDED POWDER

Aim: To prepare and submit 4 doses of eutectic powder

Type of product: Compound divided powder for internal use

Category: Carminative

Apparatus: Mortar and pestle, spatula, a white paper sheet, a sheet of butter paper

Principle: When two or more low melting point substances are mixed together, they liquefy due to the formation of a new compound which has a lower melting point than the room temperature. Such substances are called eutectic substances.

In this experiment camphor and menthol are used as carminatives. The melting point of each ingredient is lowered as a result the powder liquefies. In order to prevent liquefaction of these substances while dispensing an adsorbent such as talc is added. They are supplied in paper packets. Both camphor and menthol are eutectic in nature and also volatile in nature. Therefore, to prevent their volatilization the powder is packed in double wrapper (inner wax paper and a white paper are jointly used).

Procedure:

1. Weigh the required quantities of camphor, menthol and talc.
2. Camphor is dissolved in little quantity of alcohol in a China dish and allowed to evaporate the alcohol by stirring with a glass rod so that camphor is separated as precipitated product of fine powder (subdivided state).
3. Divide the talc into two portions.
4. To the first portion of talc add camphor and spatulate to mix evenly.
5. To the second portion of talc add menthol and spatulate to mix evenly.
6. Then prescribed amount (unit dose) of the divided powder is enclosed in double wrapper.
7. Prepare the required number of powder packet and dispense in a labelled envelope cover.

Direction:

FOR EXTERNAL USE ONLY

NOT TO BE APPLIED TO RAW OR WEEPING SURFACES

Label: Keep out of reach of infants

Storage:

Keep the powders in a well closed air tight container. Store in cool place

S. No	Ingredients	Quantity Given for 1 dose	Quantity Taken for 4 doses
1.	Camphor	1.2gm	
2.	Menthol	0.6gm	
3.	Talc	1.8gm	

Calculations

Label: (Students shall write all aspects of labelling in the space provided below)

Report:

DIVIDED POWDER		
USE: Carminative STORAGE: Keep the powders in a well closed air tight container. Store in cool place	A divided powder which contains camphor and menthol Name of the institution	Lic.no._______ Mfg. Date:____ Batch no._____ Expiry date ______

CHAPTER - 8

SUPPOSITORIES-INTRODUCTION

Suppositories are solid dosage forms designed for insertion into body orifices, typically the rectum or vagina, for localized or systemic delivery of medications. They are commonly used in the pharmaceutical and medical fields to administer drugs when other routes of administration are not feasible or desirable. Suppositories come in various shapes, sizes, and compositions, tailored to specific applications and patient needs.

Purpose: Suppositories are used for the delivery of drugs that may not be suitable for oral administration due to issues such as poor absorption, degradation in the gastrointestinal tract, or patient non-compliance. They can provide systemic effects by absorption through mucous membranes or localized effects in the rectum or vagina.

Composition: Suppositories are typically composed of active pharmaceutical ingredients (APIs) dissolved or dispersed in a suitable base or vehicle. The base serves as a carrier for the API and determines the physical characteristics of the suppository, such as its melting point, consistency, and release profile. Common bases include cocoa butter, hydrogenated vegetable oils, glycerinated gelatin, and polyethylene glycols (PEGs).

Types: There are several types of suppositories based on their composition and intended use:

Rectal Suppositories: Designed for insertion into the rectum for systemic absorption or local treatment of conditions such as constipation, hemorrhoids, or inflammatory bowel disease.

Vaginal Suppositories: Inserted into the vagina for local treatment of infections, contraception, hormone replacement therapy, or other gynecological conditions.

Urethral Suppositories: Inserted into the urethra for the treatment of urinary tract infections or erectile dysfunction.

Preparation: Suppositories are prepared using molding or compression techniques. In the molding method, the molten suppository base containing the API is poured into individual molds and allowed to solidify. Compression involves compressing powdered ingredients into suppository-shaped tablets using a tablet press. After preparation, suppositories may undergo coating or polishing to improve appearance, stability, or patient comfort.

Administration: Suppositories are administered using a dedicated applicator or inserted manually into the appropriate body orifice. Proper insertion techniques and patient education are essential to ensure safe and effective administration. After insertion, suppositories gradually melt or dissolve, releasing the medication for absorption or local action.

CHARACTERISTICS OF SUPPOSITORIES:

- It should melt at body temperature.
- It should keep its shape when being handled.
- It should release the medicament readily.
- It should be non- toxic and non – irritant to the mucous membrane.
- It should be stable on storage.

CLASSIFICATION OF SUPPOSITORIES:

Suppositories can be classified based on various criteria, including their composition, route of administration, intended use, and physical characteristics. Here's a classification of suppositories based on these factors:

Composition:

- **Fatty Base Suppositories:** These suppositories are composed primarily of fatty bases such as cocoa butter, hydrogenated vegetable oils, or glycerinated gelatin. They are suitable for both rectal and vaginal administration and are preferred for drugs that are lipophilic or require slow release.
- **Water-Soluble Base Suppositories:** These suppositories are composed of water-soluble bases such as polyethylene glycols (PEGs) or glycerinated gelatin. They are suitable for drugs that are hydrophilic or require rapid release and absorption. Water-soluble bases are often used for rectal suppositories.

Route of Administration:

- **Rectal Suppositories:** Intended for insertion into the rectum for systemic absorption or local treatment.

- **Vaginal Suppositories:** Designed for insertion into the vagina for local treatment of gynecological conditions.

Intended Use:

- **Therapeutic Suppositories:** Contain active pharmaceutical ingredients (APIs) intended to treat specific medical conditions, such as constipation, hemorrhoids, inflammation, or infections.
- **Diagnostic Suppositories:** Used for diagnostic purposes, such as rectal suppositories containing contrast agents for imaging studies or rectal thermometers for temperature measurement.
- **Prophylactic Suppositories:** Used to prevent certain medical conditions or infections, such as vaginal suppositories for contraception or prophylaxis against sexually transmitted infections.

Physical Characteristics:

- **Bullet-Shaped Suppositories:** Have a bullet-like shape with a pointed tip and rounded base, designed for ease of insertion and retention in the rectum.
- **Torpedo-Shaped Suppositories:** Have a tapered shape resembling a torpedo, designed to facilitate insertion and ensure proper placement in the rectum.
- **Oval or Elliptical Suppositories:** Have an oval or elliptical shape, suitable for both rectal and vaginal administration, with smooth edges for comfortable insertion.

Melting Point:

- **High-Melting Point Suppositories:** Formulated with fatty bases that have a higher melting point, suitable for use in tropical climates or for drugs that require slower release.
- **Low-Melting Point Suppositories:** Formulated with bases that have a lower melting point, suitable for use in temperate climates or for drugs that require rapid release and absorption.

Types of Preparation Methods for Suppositories:

Fusion or Melting Method:

- This method involves melting the suppository base, incorporating the active pharmaceutical ingredient (API), and then pouring the mixture into individual suppository molds to solidify.

- Suitable for suppository bases with a low melting point, such as cocoa butter or PEGs.
- Simple and straightforward process, suitable for heat-stable drugs.

Molding or Compression Method:

- In this method, the suppository mixture is compressed or molded into suppository-shaped tablets using a tablet press or manual compression device.
- The mixture may be prepared by blending the API with a suitable excipient or base, such as PEGs or glycerinated gelatin, and then compressing the mixture into suppository-shaped tablets.
- Suitable for drugs that are sensitive to heat or require controlled release formulations.

Hand Rolling Method:

- This method involves hand-rolling the suppository mixture into cylindrical or torpedo-shaped suppositories.
- The mixture is prepared by blending the API with a suitable excipient or base, such as cocoa butter or hydrogenated vegetable oils, and then rolling the mixture into suppository shapes.
- Suitable for small-scale compounding or when specialized equipment is not available.

Injection Molding Method:

- Injection molding involves injecting the suppository mixture into individual suppository molds using a syringe or injection device.
- The mixture may be prepared by blending the API with a suitable excipient or base, such as PEGs or glycerinated gelatin, and then injecting the mixture into suppository molds under controlled conditions.
- Suitable for large-scale production and when precise control over suppository size and shape is required.

Freeze-Drying or Lyophilization Method:

- In this method, the suppository mixture is frozen and then subjected to freeze-drying or lyophilization to remove moisture and solidify the mixture.

- The freeze-dried suppositories are then packaged and stored under controlled conditions.
- Suitable for heat-sensitive drugs or when rapid solidification is required.

Spray Drying Method:

- Spray drying involves atomizing the suppository mixture into fine droplets using a spray nozzle or atomizer and then drying the droplets in a heated chamber to form solid particles.
- The spray-dried particles are then compressed or molded into suppository-shaped tablets.
- Suitable for drugs that are sensitive to heat or require rapid solidification.
- These are some common types of preparation methods for suppositories, each offering unique advantages and considerations depending on the specific requirements of the formulation and the desired characteristics of the suppositories. The choice of preparation method depends on factors such as the properties of the drug, the desired release profile, and the scale of production.

Advantages: Suppositories offer several advantages, including:

- Avoidance of gastrointestinal degradation and first-pass metabolism.
- Rapid onset of action due to direct absorption through mucous membranes.
- Reduced risk of systemic side effects compared to oral administration.
- Convenience and ease of administration in patients unable to swallow or tolerate oral medications.

Disadvantages: Despite their advantages, suppositories may have limitations such as:

- Variation in absorption rates due to individual differences in anatomy and physiology.
- Potential discomfort or embarrassment associated with insertion.
- Need for specialized storage conditions to prevent melting or degradation of suppositories.

Date: **Experiment - 19**

GLYCERO-GELATIN SUPPOSITORY

Aim: To prepare & submit 3 Glycero-Gelatin suppositories.

Type of product: Suppository containing Glycero-Gelatin base.

Category: Rectal evacuant.

Composition: Glycero- 70%w/w, Gelatin-14%w/w.

Dose: 1gm.

Principle: Glycero-Gelatin suppository is a mixture of glycerin & water made it into stiff gelly or semi- solid consistency by adding gelatin. It contains 14%w/w of gelatin & 70%w/w of glycerol. For use in tropical climate up to 18%w/w of gelatin is generally included. Glycero-Gelatin suppositories readily dissolve in body solution & hence it is preferable to a fatty base for incorporating medicaments like antiseptics. The rate of release of drug from these suppositories is for a prolonged period. These suppositories may take 40min to dissolve in water at 37^0C. The Glycerin in the preparation acts as a laxative by stimulating rectum which is due to its mild irritant action. The gelatin for the preparation is of Pharma grade A or B to prevent the incompatibilities in the preparation due to the acids like Tannic acid. It acts as gelling agent thereby render the preparation into semi-solid consistency. Both these ingredients have water holding properties and also have softening & lubricant property. Purified water is used to soften the gelatin & to hasten its dissolution in glycerin. The presence of water also minimizes the dehydrating effects of glycerol-gelatin suppositories.

Procedure:

1. The mould is cleaned with hot water or detergent.
2. The mould is lubricated with either liquid paraffin or arachis oil.
3. Then the mould is inverted on the ice.
4. Accurately weigh quantity of glycerol is transferred into a beaker and heated to 100^0C& prevent the evaporation of glycerol.
5. Disperse the powdered gelatin in little quantity of water taken in a porcelain dish. Add the hot glycerol to the contents of the porcelain dish & stir it to mix uniformly & weigh it and then transfer on to the boiling water bath.

6. Heat it for about 15minutes until solution is complete. Stir often gently to prevent entrapment of air bubbles.
7. When the solution is complete, weigh the dish & the contents. If necessary, evaporate and add hot water to obtain the correct weight.
8. Pour the hot molten mass into cavities of chilled moulds after skimming & remove any entrapped air bubbles softening to muslin in a warm strainer.
9. Keep the mould in an ice bath & refrigerate for half-an-hour to solidify the mass inthe cavities.
10. Unscrew the mould to open. Suppositories are removed & excess of lubricant on thesurface of the suppositories are removed with a blotting paper.
11. Select the best suppositories. Each suppository is wrapped with a butter paperseparately.
12. Suppositories are dispensed in a neatly labelled box or wide mouthed bottle.

Formulation table:

S. No	Ingredients For blank Glycero gelatin suppositories	Quantity as per IP For 100 parts	Quantity taken for each 1gm suppository	Quantity required for 6 suppositories each weighing 1gm
1	Glycerin	70 parts	70/100 x 1=	70/100 x 6 =
2	Gelatin	14 parts	14/100x 1=	14/100 x 6 =
3	Water	16 parts	16/100 x 1=	16/100 x 6 =

Storage: Store in a cool and dark place.

Special instruction: For rectal use only.

Report:

Date: **Experiment - 20**

COCOA BUTTER SUPPOSITORY

Aim: To prepare and submit 6 Cocoa butter suppositories containing chloral hydrate.

Type of product: Cocoa butter suppository containing soluble solid.

Category: Sedative- Hypnotic.

Composition: Chloral hydrate – 6% w/w

Dose: 1gm

Principle:

These are cocoa butter suppositories, containing soluble solids like chloral hydrate. The melting point of cocoa butter depresses which leads to the difficulty in the insertion as it becomes soft when patient holds it between the fingers. Limit of soluble solids is up to 2.5% w/w. Above this limit, soluble solids will affect the melting point of the base. To solve this problem, use of synthetic bases having higher melting points e.g., massa estranium or Witepsol can be used or the addition of white bees' wax, provides the M.P. of the suppository not exceeding the body temperature.

Suppositories are prepared in moulds. Lubricating the mould facilities easy removal of suppositories. The cold mould is used for dissipating the heat content of suppository mass and hastening setting.

When cocoa butter is heated above its melting temperature (about 36^0C) and chilled to its solidification point (below 15^0C), cocoa butter attains a melting point of about 24^0C (immediately after returning to room temperature). It means that cocoa butter is liquid at room temperature. Therefore, cocoa butter must not be heated at higher temperature. Lubrication of mould is necessary because, cocoa butter has the tendency of sticking to the sides of the mould.

The mould is overfilled with homogeneous dispersion of drug and base. This is because, while cooling, the base contracts forming hollow depression at the center top of the suppository. Overfilling the mould prevents the formation of hollow depression. The displacement value of boric acid is 1.5. Using displacement value, weight of cocoa butter is calculated.

Formulation table:

S. No	Ingredients	Quantity Given	Quantity Taken	Purpose
1	Chloral hydrate	60mg		Sedative & Hypnotic
2	Cocoa butter	q.s to 1gm		Suppository base

Procedure:

1. Calculations:

a DRUG: For 8 suppositories (2 extra)

***Formula*:**

Medicament required = Amount of drug x Total number of suppositories

Medicament required = 60 x 8 =480 mg or 0.48 gm

a. Displacement value = 1.5

b. BASE:

***Formula*:**

Base displaced = Weight of suppository x Amount of drug required / Displacement value of the drug

Cocoa butter displaced by 480mg of drug = 1 x 480 / 1.5 = 320mg or 0.32gm

c. Required cocoa butter base

***Formula*:**

Amount of base = (Total number of suppositories x weight of suppository) – total amount of base displaced = (8 x 1) - 0.32 = 7.680

d. So, the ***working formula*** becomes

1. *Chloral hydrate-480 mg and cocoa butter base-7.68gm*
2. The mould is cleaned with hot water and detergent.
3. Weigh required amounts of drug (passed through 100 mesh) and cocoa butter.
4. Select a dry, clean mold and place it on a clean tile.
5. Shred the cocoa butter in a small beaker or porcelain dish.

6. Put finely powdered drug on a clean warm tile.
7. Place the beaker containing cocoa butter on the water bath until about 2/3rd of the content gets melted and then takes out from the water bath. The rest of the amount ismelted with constant stirring.
8. Pour about half of the melted base on to the medicament on the warm tile and startlevigating as quickly as possible.
9. Transfer the dispersion to the remaining melted base in the beaker and stir to formhomogenous mixture.
10. Continue stirring until the mixture begins to thicken and then fill each cavity of themold to overflowing.
11. Leave for 2 or 3 minutes until the mass just set and then remove the excess from themold with a sharp knife or a blade.
12. Leave the mold in a cool place for 10 – 15min (ice bath).
13. Finally open the mold and tap it slowly on tissue paper.
14. Wrap each suppository in a butter paper lined with lubricant and pack in partitioned box.

Special instruction: For rectal use only.

Storage: Store in a cool place.

Report:

Date: **Experiment - 21**

ZINC OXIDE SUPPOSITORY

Aim: To prepare and submit 5 Zinc oxide suppositories.

Type of product: Cocoa butter suppository containing insoluble solid.

Category: Local anti-infective

Composition: Zinc oxide – 12% w/w

Dose: 1gm

Direction: One suppository is to be used.

Principle: These suppositories contain insoluble solids like boric acid, which acts as anti- infective agent. Zinc oxide is insoluble in water as well s in cocoa butter and therefore it must be dispersed in cocoa butter, a suppository base. Suppositories are prepared in moulds. Lubricating the mould facilitates easy removal of suppositories. The cold mould is used for dissipating the heat content of suppository mass and hastening setting.

When cocoa butter is heated above its melting temperature (about 36^0C) and chilled to its solidification point (below 15^0C), cocoa butter attains a melting point of about 24^0C (immediately after returning to room temperature). It means that cocoa butter is liquid atroom temperature. Therefore, cocoa butter must not be heated at higher temperature. Lubrication of mould is necessary because, cocoa butter has the tendency of sticking to the sides of the mould.

Warmed tile is used to disperse the drug in the base. This prevents the rapid cooling and solidification of base during mixing. The mould is overfilled with homogeneous dispersion ofdrug and base. This is because, while cooling, the base contracts forming hollow depressionat the center top of the suppository. Overfilling the mould prevents the formation of hollow depression. The displacement value of boric acid is 1.5. Using displacement value, weight of cocoa butter is calculated.

Each mould can accommodate 6 suppositories. Therefore, six suppositories are prepared. One suppository mass extra (quantity) is calculated, in order to compensate the loss during preparation. One suppository mass extra is necessary in order to compensate the loss due to overfilling of the mould cavity. Therefore, the working formula is calculated for 8 suppositories (6+1+1).

Formula:

S. No	Ingredients	Quantity Given	Quantity Taken	Purpose
1	Zinc oxide	120mg		Anti-infective
2	Cocoa butter	q.s to 1gm		Suppository base

Procedure:

1. **Calculations:**

DRUG: For 8 suppositories (2 extra)

Formula:

Medicament required = Amount of drug x Total number of suppositories

Medicament required = 120 x 8 =960 mg or 0.96 gm

Displacement value= 1.5

BASE:

Formula:

*Base displaced = Weight of suppository * Amount of drug required / Displacement value of the drug*

Cocoa butter displaced by 480mg of drug = 1 x 960 / 1.5 = 640mg or 0.64gmRequired cocoa butter base

Formula:

Amount of base = (Total number of suppositories x weight of suppository) –total amount of base displaced = (8 x 1) - 0.64 = 7.36

So the ***working formula*** becomes

Zinc oxide -*0.64 gm and cocoa butter base-7.36gm*

1. The mould is cleaned with hot water and detergent.
2. Weigh required amounts of drug (passed through 100 mesh) and cocoa butter
3. Select a dry, clean mold and place it on a clean tile
4. Shred the cocoa butter in a small beaker or porcelain dish

5. Put finely powdered drug on a clean warm tile
6. Place the beaker containing cocoa butter on the water bath until about 2/3rd of the content gets melted and then takes out from the water bath. The rest of theamount is melted with constant stirring
7. Pour about half of the melted base on to the medicament on the warm tile andstart levigating as quickly as possible
8. Transfer the dispersion to the remaining melted base in the beaker and stir toform homogenous mixture
9. Continue stirring until the mixture begins to thicken and then fill each cavityof the mold to overflowing
10. Leave for 2 or 3 minutes until the mass just set and then remove the excessfrom the mold with a sharp knife or a blade
11. Leave the mold in a cool place for 10 – 15min (ice bath)
12. Finally open the mold and tap it slowly on tissue paper
13. Wrap each suppository in a butter paper lined with lubricant and pack in partitioned box.

Special instruction: For rectal use only.

Storage: Store in a cool place.

Report

CHAPTER - 9

SEMISOLIDS – INTRODUCTION

Semisolids are pharmaceutical dosage forms that exhibit a semi-solid consistency, typically containing a mixture of solid and liquid phases. They are widely used in topical applications for the treatment of various dermatological conditions and localized symptoms. Semisolid dosage forms include creams, ointments, gels, pastes, and lotions, each offering unique properties and advantages for specific therapeutic purposes.

COMPOSITION:

- Semisolids are composed of a combination of solid and liquid components, along with various excipients and additives.
- Solid components may include active pharmaceutical ingredients (APIs), such as drugs or therapeutic agents, as well as solid excipients like waxes, fatty acids, or polymers.
- Liquid components may include solvents, vehicles, or penetration enhancers, such as water, oils, alcohols, glycols, or surfactants.
- Excipients such as emulsifiers, stabilizers, preservatives, thickeners, and antioxidants are added to improve stability, consistency, texture, and efficacy.

TYPES OF SEMISOLIDS:

Creams: Emulsions of oil and water phases, typically containing higher water content than ointments. Creams are easily spreadable and absorb quickly into the skin.

Ointments: Hydrophobic or oleaginous preparations containing higher amounts of oil or fatty substances. Ointments provide occlusive and protective effects and are suitable for delivering lipophilic drugs.

Gels: Semi-solid colloidal dispersions containing gelling agents or polymers that provide a gel-like consistency. Gels are often transparent or translucent and offer enhanced drug release and skin adherence.

Pastes: Thick, viscous preparations containing high concentrations of solid particles dispersed in a semi-solid base. Pastes provide a protective barrier and are used for treating skin conditions such as eczema or psoriasis.

Lotions: Fluid, pourable preparations containing higher amounts of water than oil. Lotions are lightweight and non-greasy and are suitable for covering large skin areas.

Preparation:

- Semisolids are typically prepared by incorporating the API and other ingredients into a suitable base or vehicle using mixing, blending, or homogenization techniques.
- Emulsification methods, such as high-shear mixing or homogenization, are used to prepare creams and gels by dispersing oil and water phases into a stable emulsion.
- Heating and cooling cycles may be employed to melt or solidify the semisolid base and achieve the desired consistency and texture.
- Quality control tests, including viscosity measurement, pH determination, stability testing, and microbiological analysis, are conducted to ensure the quality, safety, and efficacy of the final product.

Classification of Ointment Bases:

Oleaginous Bases: Composed primarily of greasy or oily substances, such as hydrocarbons (e.g., petrolatum, mineral oil), vegetable oils (e.g., almond oil, olive oil), or animal fats (e.g., lanolin, beeswax). Oleaginous bases provide occlusive and protective effects and are suitable for lipophilic drugs.

Absorption Bases: Contain a combination of water-in-oil (W/O) emulsifying agents and oleaginous components, allowing for the incorporation of aqueous solutions or dispersions. Examples include hydrophilic petrolatum and absorption ointment bases.

Water-Removable Bases: Contain a mixture of oleaginous components and water-soluble surfactants or emulsifiers, allowing for easy removal with water. These bases are suitable for water-soluble drugs and include hydrophilic ointment bases.

Water-Soluble Bases: Composed primarily of water-soluble substances, such as polyethylene glycols (PEGs) or glycerin. Water-soluble bases are suitable for drugs that are soluble or dispersible in water and provide a non-greasy, easy-to-remove formulation.

Application:

- Semisolids are applied topically to the skin or mucous membranes for localized treatment of dermatological conditions, wounds, infections, inflammation, pain, or other symptoms.
- Proper application techniques, such as gentle rubbing or spreading, are employed to ensure even distribution and absorption of the semisolid preparation.
- Patient education regarding the frequency, duration, and proper application of semisolids is essential to ensure optimal therapeutic outcomes and minimize adverse effects.

Preparation of Ointments:

The ointments can be prepared by the following method.

Fusion or Melting Method:

- This method involves melting the ointment base and incorporating the active pharmaceutical ingredient (API) and other ingredients into the molten base.
- Suitable for ointment bases with a high melting point, such as white petrolatum or beeswax.
- The API is added to the molten base and mixed thoroughly to ensure uniform dispersion.
- The mixture is then allowed to cool and solidify at room temperature or under controlled cooling conditions.

Geometric Dilution Method:

- This method is used when preparing ointments containing potent APIs that require careful mixing to achieve uniform distribution.
- The API and other powdered ingredients are mixed in geometrically increasing proportions to ensure thorough blending and uniform dispersion.
- The mixture is then incorporated into the ointment base using the fusion method or other suitable techniques.

Solvent Evaporation Method:

- This method is used for preparing ointments containing volatile or heat-sensitive APIs.

- The API is dissolved or dispersed in a suitable solvent or vehicle, such as alcohol, glycerin, or propylene glycol.
- The solvent is then evaporated under reduced pressure or at elevated temperatures to leave behind a dry residue of the API, which is then incorporated into the ointment base.

Trituration Method:

- This method is used for preparing ointments containing insoluble or poorly soluble APIs.
- The API is triturated or ground with a small amount of the ointment base to form a smooth paste or suspension.
- The paste or suspension is then gradually incorporated into the remaining ointment base while mixing to achieve uniform dispersion.

Emulsification Method:

- This method is used for preparing emulsion-based ointments, such as water-in-oil (W/O) or oil-in-water (O/W) emulsions.
- The API is dissolved or dispersed in one phase of the emulsion, typically the oil phase for W/O emulsions or the aqueous phase for O/W emulsions.
- The two phases are then emulsified together using high-shear mixing or homogenization to form a stable emulsion, which is then incorporated into the ointment base.

Direct Incorporation Method:

- This method involves directly incorporating the API and other ingredients into the ointment base without prior mixing or preparation.
- Suitable for ointment bases that are soft or pliable enough to allow for easy blending and dispersion of the API and other ingredients.

Storage: Store in a cool place and away from sunlight as it melts at higher temperature.

Auxiliary label:

FOR EXTERNAL USE ONLY.

Date: **Experiment -22**

SULPHUR OINTMENT

Aim: To prepare and submit Sulphur ointment.

Principle: Sulphur is an insoluble solid which is incorporated in simple ointment. Simple ointment without medicament is used as an emollient. Oily type of bases provides more penetration. To increase the consistency hard paraffin is used. Wool fat, Ceto stearyl alcohol, white soft paraffin was used as base components.

Procedure:

1. Accurately weigh all the ingredients and transfer them to a porcelain dish.
2. Allow them to melt on water bath by Stirring gently with a glass rod to aid melting.
3. Transfer the required amount of Sulphur.
4. Place it on a ointment tile. Levigate the powder homogenously without any lumps gradually by incorporating the melted base using ointment spatula.
5. Transfer the ointment into the final wide mouthed container and close with a tight closure.

Use: Antiseptic (In the treatment of scabies and acne)

Directions:

APPLY AS DIRECTED

FOR EXTERNAL USE ONLY

Storage: KEEP IN A WELL – CLOSED CONTAINER IN A COOL PLACE.

Formulation table:

S.No	Ingredients	Quantity Given for 100g	Quantity Taken
1.	Sublimed Sulphur	10g	
2.	Wool fat	4.5g	
3.	Hard paraffin	4.5g	
4.	Ceto stearyl alcohol	4.5g	
5.	White soft paraffin	86.5g	

Calculations

Label:

(Students shall write all aspects of labelling in the space provided below)

SULPHUR OINTMENT		
USE: Antiseptic (In the treatment of scabies and acne) **STORAGE:** keep in a well – closed container in a cool place.	Ointment which contains sublimed Sulphur Name of the institution	Lic.no.________ Mfg. Date:_____ Batch no._______ Expiry date ____

Report:

Date: **Experiment -23**

NON-STAINING IODINE OINTMENT WITH METHYL SAILICYLATE

Aim: To prepare and submit 10grams of non-staining iodine ointment with methyl salicylate.

Category: ointment.

Principle: Iodine is a counter irritant. The iodine ointment due to their staining property, have poor cosmetic acceptability. The non-staining iodine ointment contains no free iodine, and therefore it does not stain. The unsaturated higher fatty acids are allowed to react with iodine producing non-staining product.

$$CH_3(CH_2)_2 - CH = CH - (CH_2)_7 - COOH + I_2 \rightarrow CH_3(CH_2)_7 - CHI - CHI(CH_2)_7 + COOH$$

The reactants are allowed to interact in closed vessel occasionally. When the product turnsgreenish black, it is tested for non-staining property.

The iodine undergoes sublimation if reaction is carried in open vessel. Iodine is insoluble andto ensure uniform mixing the vessel should be shaken occasionally. Though the product is greenish black it is non-staining in nature. The reaction usually requires 1 hour of time for completion. Since iodine is coloured, soft paraffin is used as a base. Methyl salicylate is counter irritant and since it is volatile, it should be added in non-staining iodine ointment at 40-45°C.

Apparatus: Porcelain dish, glass rod, water bath.

Procedure:

1. Crush the iodine using glass mortar and pestle.
2. Heat the mixture of arachis oil – iodine in a closed vessel at a temperature of 50-60°Cwith occasional shaking. When the product is greenish-black, take the vessel away from its heating source and check the product for non-staining property.
3. Melt soft paraffin on water bath in a porcelain dish. Add the reaction mixture to themelted paraffin and stir until solidification.

Container and storage: Store in iodine resistant wide mouth bottle. Store in well closed container in cool place.

Precaution: DO NOT APPLY ON BROKEN SKIN

Category: Counter irritant

Formulation table:

S. No	Ingredients	Quantity Given for 100g	Quantity Taken
1.	Iodine	5g	
2.	Arachis oil	15ml	
3.	Soft paraffin	100gm to make	
4.	Methyl salicylate	5ml	

Calculations

Label:

(Students shall write all aspects of labelling in the space provided below)

NON-STAINING IODINE OINTMENT WITH METHYL SAILICYLATE		
USE: Counter irritant STORAGE: Store in iodine resistant wide mouth bottle. Store in well closed container in cool place.	Ointment which iodine and soft paraffin Name of the institution	Lic.no.________ Mfg. Date:_____ Batch no.______ Expiry date ____

Report:

Date: **Experiment - 24**

CARBOPOL GEL

Aim: To prepare and submit Carbopol gel.

Principle: Gels are semisolid preparations made using substances called gelling agents. These agents undergo a high degree of cross-linking, which affects the viscosity of the dispersed phase by restricting the movement of the dispersing medium. Gels contain high proportion of water (70-90%), therefore they are easily applied and washed away from the skin surfaces. Gels are transparent which imparts elegance to preparations. Carbomer is a generic name to the polymer known as Carbopol. Carbomer require a neutralizer or a pH adjusting chemical to create the gel after the gelling agent has been wetted in the dispersion medium, Carbopol from acidic aqueous solutions of pH3.0. They thicken at higher pH 5-6. Carbopol is very hygroscopic (quickly absorbs moisture from atmosphere).Citric acid is added to maintain pH around 3 for better dispersion of polymer and disodium EDTA is added to sequester metal ions present in the water which otherwise interfere in swelling of Carbopol.

Apparatus: Beakers, measuring cylinder, volumetric flask, over hood stirrer/ magnetic stirrer,porcelain dish, glass rod.

Procedure:

1. Weigh Carbopol in dry conditions.
2. In 50% of water dissolve citric acid and disodium EDTA.
3. Disperse Carbopol vigorously in above solution using spatula or overhead stirrer foraround 30 minutes.
4. Keep aside the dispersed polymer for 10 minutes.
5. Add the mixture of glycerine, sodium benzoate in remaining quantity of water intopolymer mixture and mix it homogenously.
6. Neutralize the above mixture using 10% NaOH Upto pH 7.
7. Check the pH after each addition of NaOH using pH paper.

Formulation table:

S. No	Ingredients	Quantity Given for 100g	Quantity Taken
1.	Carbopol 980	1.2g	
2.	Citric acid	1g	
3.	Disodium EDTA	0.1g	
4.	Glycerine	5ml	
5.	Sodium benzoate	0.18g	
6.	Water soluble colorant	q.s	
7.	10% sodium hydroxide solution	q.s	
8.	Purified water	100ml	

Calculations

Label:

(Students shall write all aspects of labelling in the space provided below)

CARBOPOL GEL		
USE: Gelling agent STORAGE: Store in closed and cool places	Gel which contains Carbopol 980 Name of the institution	Lic.no.________ Mfg. Date:_____ Batch no.______ Expiry date ____

Report:

CHAPTER - 10

GARGLES AND MOUTHWASH'S INTRODUCTION

Gargles and mouthwashes are liquid preparations used for oral hygiene, dental care, and treatment of various oral conditions. They are intended to be swished or gargled in the mouth and then expelled or spit out. These formulations are commonly used to freshen breath, reduce plaque and gingivitis, soothe oral irritations, and treat conditions such as mouth ulcers, sore throat, and halitosis (bad breath).

Composition:

- Gargles and mouthwashes typically contain a combination of active ingredients, excipients, and flavoring agents.
- Active ingredients may include antimicrobial agents (e.g., chlorhexidine, metylpyridinium chloride), analgesics (e.g., benzocaine, lidocaine), anti-inflammatory agents (e.g., steroids), astringents (e.g., witch hazel), and/or antiseptics (e.g., hydrogen peroxide, iodine).
- Excipients are used to adjust the pH, viscosity, and stability of the formulation. These may include water, alcohol (e.g., ethanol or isopropyl alcohol), glycerin, sorbitol, surfactants, and buffering agents.
- Flavoring agents such as mint, menthol, eucalyptus, or citrus oils are often added to improve taste and provide a refreshing sensation.

TYPES:

Antiseptic Mouthwashes: Contain antimicrobial agents to reduce bacteria and plaque buildup in the mouth, promoting oral hygiene and preventing dental caries and gum disease.

Analgesic Mouthwashes: Contain pain-relieving agents to alleviate discomfort from sore throat, mouth ulcers, or dental procedures.

Anti-inflammatory Mouthwashes: Contain anti-inflammatory agents to reduce inflammation and soothe oral irritations caused by conditions such as gingivitis or mucositis.

Astringent Mouthwashes: Contain astringent agents to tighten and tone oral tissues, providing relief from minor bleeding or inflammation of the gums.

PREPARATION:

- Gargles and mouthwashes are prepared by mixing the active ingredients, excipients, and flavoring agents in appropriate proportions.
- The ingredients are dissolved or dispersed in a suitable solvent, such as water or alcohol, and may be adjusted to achieve the desired concentration and pH.
- Quality control tests, including pH measurement, viscosity determination, microbial testing, and stability studies, are conducted to ensure the safety, efficacy, and stability of the final product.

Application:

- Gargles and mouthwashes are used by pouring a small amount into the mouth, swishing or gargling for a specified duration (usually 30 seconds to 1 minute), and then spitting out the solution.
- They may be used as part of daily oral hygiene routines, after brushing and flossing, or as needed to alleviate specific oral symptoms.
- Some formulations may require dilution with water before use, depending on the concentration and intended use of the product.

FORMULATION:

The formulation of gargles and mouthwashes involves creating liquid preparations that are intended for oral hygiene, breath freshening, or treatment of oral conditions such as gingivitis or sore throat. These formulations typically contain active ingredients, flavoring agents, preservatives, and other excipients to provide the desired therapeutic effects and sensory attributes.

Active Ingredients:

- **Antimicrobial Agents:** Such as chlorhexidine, methylpyridinium chloride, or essential oils (e.g., thymol, menthol, eucalyptol) to help reduce oral bacteria and prevent plaque buildup.
- **Analgesics:** Such as benzocaine or lidocaine to provide temporary relief from oral pain or sore throat.

- **Astringents:** Such as alum or tannic acid to help tighten and soothe irritated oral tissues.
- **Anti-inflammatory Agents**: Such as nonsteroidal anti-inflammatory drugs (NSAIDs) or corticosteroids to reduce inflammation and discomfort in the mouth or throat.

Flavoring Agents:

- **Essential Oils:** Such as peppermint, spearmint, or wintergreen oil, which provide a refreshing taste and help mask the medicinal flavor of active ingredients.
- **Artificial Flavors:** Such as fruit flavors (e.g., cherry, berry, citrus) or sweeteners (e.g., saccharin, sorbitol) to enhance palatability and encourage regular use.

Solvents and Vehicles:

- **Water:** Typically, the main component of gargles and mouthwashes, serving as the solvent for active ingredients and other components.
- **Alcohol:** Such as ethanol or isopropanol, which act as solvents, preservatives, and vehicles for active ingredients. Alcohol also provides a refreshing sensation and helps to dissolve flavoring agents and essential oils.
- **Glycerin:** Used as a humectant to prevent drying of oral tissues and to provide a soothing feel.
- **Propylene Glycol:** Another humectant commonly used in mouthwash formulations to help maintain moisture and viscosity.

Preservatives and Stabilizers:

- **Benzoic Acid, Sodium Benzoate, or Potassium Sorbate:** Common preservatives used to prevent microbial growth and ensure product stability.
- **Sodium Bicarbonate or Citric Acid**: Used as buffering agents to adjust the pH of the formulation and maintain stability.

Surfactants:

- **Polysorbate 20 or Polysorbate 80:** Nonionic surfactants used to emulsify and disperse essential oils and other lipophilic ingredients in the aqueous phase of the formulation.

Additional Excipients:

- **Thickening Agents:** Such as carboxymethylcellulose (CMC) or xanthan gum, which help to increase viscosity and provide a smooth consistency.
- **Colorants:** Optional ingredients used to enhance the appearance of the product.
- **Sweeteners:** Additional sweetening agents may be added to improve taste and palatability, especially in formulations targeted towards pediatric or sensitive populations.

Labeling: The label should include use only as directed. Avoid contact with the eyes. NOT TOBE SWALLOWED. Dilute with warm water.

Direction: Dilution with warm water before use.

Storage: Store at room temperature away from sunlight.

Date: **Experiment - 25**

IODINE GARGLE

Aim: To prepare and submit iodine gargle.

Principle: Gargles are clear aqueous solutions of medicaments in concentrated form used in the treatment of throat infections. They bring the medicaments in close contact with the mucous membrane of the throat, only for the short time. They must be fast acting and pleasantly flavour. Iodine gargle contains 0.1% free iodine which shows antiseptic action and maintains oral hygiene. It is mainly used in pre and post oral surgeries to clean the oral cavity. Povidone iodine complex is composed of poly vinyl pyrrolidone and iodine in 90:10. Glycerin aids in soothing action, sucrose acts as taste masker providing sweet taste. Peppermint water is a flavoured vehicle.

Apparatus: Beaker, glass rod, Glass mortar and pestle.

Procedure:

Dissolve polyvinyl pyrrolidone and iodine in peppermint water. Then add glycerine, sucrose and mix well to get a clear homogenous solution.

Formulation table:

S. No	Ingredients	Quantity Given for 100g	Quantity Taken
1.	Polyvinyl pyrrolidone	90mg	
2.	Iodine	10mg	
3.	Glycerine	4ml	
4.	Sucrose	0.5gm	
5.	Peppermint water	100ml q.s	

Calculations

Label: (Students shall write all aspects of labelling in the space provided below)

IODINE GARGLE		
USE: Treatment of throat infections STORAGE: Store in closed and cool places	Iodine gargle contains 0.1% free iodine Name of the institution	Lic.no._______ Mfg. Date:____ Batch no._____ Expiry date ___

Report:

Date: **Experiment - 26**

CHLORHEXIDINE MOUTHWASH

Aim: To prepare and submit chlorhexidine gluconate mouthwash

Principle: Chlorhexidine gluconate is used as an antiseptic. It has immediate bactericidal andprolonged bacteriostatic actions. It is harmful at high concentrations but safe at low concentrations. It is incorporated as a solution. Sodium fluoride is used to enhance the strength of teeth, by the formation of fluorapatite (a naturally occurring component of tooth enamel) it protects against tooth decay and prevents cavities

Zinc chloride is used as an astringent, coloring agent gives attractive colour to the preparation, mint flavour forms flavoured aqueous base.

Apparatus: Beaker, glass rod, measuring cylinder.

Procedure:

1. Dissolve sodium fluoride and zinc chloride in 3/4th of water.
2. Add chlorhexidine gluconate solution and colorant and mix well.
3. Add sufficient water to make the required volume.

Category: Antiseptic and anti-plaque

Use: It is used to enhance oral hygiene and to prevent or combat gum diseases such as gingivitis

Storage: Store in cool and dark place

Formulation table:

S. No	Ingredients	Quantity Given for 100g	Quantity Taken
1.	Chlorhexidine gluconate	0.2g	
2.	Sodium fluoride	0.05g	
3.	Zinc chloride	0.09g	

Table Contd...

4.	Colouring agent	q.s	
5.	Flavoured purified water	100ml q.s	

Calculations:

Label: (Students shall write all aspects of labelling in the space provided below)

CHLORHEXIDINE MOUTHWASH		
USE: Antiseptic and anti-plaque STORAGE: Store in cool and dark place	A mouth wash contains chlorhexidine gluconate Name of the institution	Lic.no.________ Mfg. Date:______ Batch no.________ Expiry date _______

Report:

www.ingramcontent.com/pod-product-compliance
Lightning Source LLC
Chambersburg PA
CBHW071225230926
51849CB00001B/28
* 9 7 8 9 3 4 8 7 3 4 7 1 6 *